Beco
True Athlete

A Practical Philosophy for Flourishing through Sport

Laurence Cassøe Halsted

First published in 2021 by Sequoia Books

ISBN
Print: 9781914110030
EPUB: 9781914110047

A CIP record for this book is available from the British Library

Library of Congress Cataloguing-In-Publication Data
Name: Laurence Halsted, author
Title: Becoming a True Athlete: A Practical Philosophy for Flourishing Through Sport
Description: 1st Edition, Sequoia Books UK 2021
Print: 9781914110030
EPUB: 9781914110047

Library of Congress Control Number: 2021914116

Print and Electronic production managed by Deanta Global

Cover design by Kelly Miller

Dedication

Dedicated to my two mentees thus far, Ryan and Souley.
You have given me far more than you can know.

Overview

Part 3   Mental-Emotional Strategies and Practices for Cultivating the True Athlete Virtues

Prologue

This book encapsulates the experiences and passion of a wide range of contributors, but it also represents a culmination of my own transformational adventures in sport. My story is not unusual, considering that every athlete who stays the course long enough will come out the other end inextricably changed compared to the youth that began their journey. I consider myself lucky that through the people I got to work with as a two-time Olympian, and the chances that came my way, I was able to experience certain key moments that allowed me to view with fresh eyes not only my own performance but the whole of sport itself. Some things were learnt slowly through repetition, but others came more like revelations, changing my perspective seemingly overnight. It is these such revelations – a highly personal exploration with a sport psychologist in a dark time of injury, a conversation on the meaning of sport with my wife, being introduced to a new approach to team dynamics and performance – that lit the path towards writing this book. My primary motivation for writing it is to help athletes have a more positive experience of sport, to help them avoid some of the most unnecessary pitfalls and to recognise the meaningful aspects of their journey more clearly. I am also excited to present a vision for how sports culture could look and feel on the ground if we are to unlock its true potential for doing good in the world.

Growing up, my life revolved around sport and my main sport was fencing. Both my parents were Olympic fencers, and they supported me in every way I could have hoped for. I was one of those athletes who took losing to heart. As a kid I would be in floods of tears after being knocked out of youth tournaments, feeling down for days or sometimes even weeks after the event. The final time I cried after a defeat was when I was 24 years old and competing in a senior World Cup, the highest standard of tournament below the World Championships and Olympics. I remember walking out of the competition hall in a nondescript suburb of Bonn, Germany, feeling devastated and worthless. It was grey and drizzling rain. I felt like quitting. Things were not going to plan. I felt so far from achieving my dream of following my mum and dad in competing at the Olympics. The truth is that although I was representing my country at senior level and had some decent results under my belt, I had hardly developed my mindset or approach since my junior years. Looking back, I'm not very proud of my younger self. At the time I was arro-gant and self-centred – hard working in some ways but mostly hedonistic. My competitive mindset was fierce, but also aggres-sive and hostile. I felt a strong dislike for my opponents and frequently disrespected my compatriots. I see now that much of this was born out of a fear of inadequacy and failure. In my final junior year, at 19 years of age and one of the most experienced in the British junior team, I was sent home in disgrace from the World Championships in Bulgaria after a riotous night that I would rather forget. Certainly, no kind of role model.

Flash forward to the end of my fencing career, hanging up my swords at the age of 32, as a double Olympian, I now had a dramatically altered perspective of the value and meaning of sport and the attitudes and behaviours that help or hinder you as an athlete. Even more importantly, I had a clear idea of *how* I had arrived there.

For one thing, between my two Olympics in 2012 and 2016, I had taken a two-year break from serious training and competition. The reason for that break was that the lead-up to qualifying for the London Olympics in 2012 was the hardest and most stressful period in my career. The Olympic year began in nightmare fashion, with my first ever major injury – breaking the wrist on my sword-arm, which required two surgeries and four months without being able to hold a weapon. The battle to get back to fitness and claim the spot in the Olympic team that I felt was rightfully mine was plagued by fear, bitterness and envy towards my teammates. But this was also where I started working with a wonderful sport psychologist, Katie Warriner, who helped me discover a powerful new perspective – one that is based on striving to live by my values. This period proved to be a major turning point in my life. Having clawed my way back into the team and competed in my hometown Olympic Games (an indescribable, thrilling ride that very few athletes have the fortune and privilege to experience), I decided to take an extended break from the sport to give space to some, as yet, unexplored parts of me. I travelled through South America to practice my Spanish, visited my sister and her family in Australia and spent four exhilarating months on an outdoor leadership course deep in the Canadian wilderness. One year away from competitive fencing led to two as I met my future wife on one of my stops, in Copenhagen, Denmark, where I set up a new life in a new country with her. The fire to return for another shot at the Olympics eventually returned and with it came a fresh approach, founded on the new perspective I had gained during my time away. This would be all about ensuring quality, not merely quantity in my training, and the joy of giving my best in competition and of being part of an ambitious team with huge potential. When performing I felt free of self-judgement, and I had a greater sense of, and appreciation for, the path I was choosing to take this time around. I was clear on why I was doing it and had the mental tools and strategies to help me stick to my game-plan in competition, and to live by my values along the way. I also knew that this would be the final act in my fencing career, and that motivated me to prepare for what would come afterwards.

At the Rio de Janeiro Olympics in 2016, during my debut in the individual event, on the biggest stage and under the glaring spotlights, I got off to a disastrous start – within three minutes, I was 8-1 down to my Chinese opponent in a match to 15 points. It looked like it could become a whitewash. My younger self would have been flooded by fear and anxiety at the prospect of a humiliating loss. However, the work I had done in the intervening years meant that I felt free of any suffocating emotions. I simply maintained a calm, yet fierce, determination to fight my way back into the match. I didn't win that match, but I came right back in it, and it is one of the performances I am most proud of. There was a stark contrast between how it felt to compete free of anxiety and how it felt to compete with nervousness and inconsistency, which plagued the majority of my career. It showed me the immense power of the strategies and techniques I learnt along the way. For too long I had been far too focussed on the outcome of my performances and knew little of what the *process* should look and feel like. I also misattributed the value of what I was engaged in – thinking that my results in the sport would alone define whether I was successful, whether it was all meaningful, or not.

As I got older and my international competitors became good friends (I learnt to break free of the protective armour that prevented me from appreciating them as people), I realised that none of them were satisfied with what they had achieved:

those in the top 100 wanted to get to the top 20; world champions desperately wanted to be Olympic champions; Olympic champions wanted to defend their title. It is the nature of sport – and of athletes – to always feel you could have done more, or done better. But if it is inevitable that *everyone*, regardless of the level they reach, will end up somewhat unsatisfied with their achievements, then what really is the point of it all? The real point, I came to realise, is in the development of the self, in the relationships you build and incredible experiences you share with people from all over the world, in the positive impact you can have on others. The point truly *is* the joy of effort, of overcoming challenge and the pursuit of personal excellence. If you cannot find meaning in those places, then you will not find it anywhere.

My experiences led me to speak out on what I saw as competitive sport leading participants down a misleading path and then failing to deliver on its mythical promises – promises which often turned out to be misguided in the first place. That in turn brought me into contact with some like-minded people who were equally eager to explore what a better culture of sport could look like and to help bring it back on track. People such as Sam Parfitt, a former elite tennis player and athletic director with an inspired vision for what sport can represent, and Pam Boteler, a top American canoe athlete who was the first woman to beat men in the US nationals as well as the driving force behind the movement to bring gender equality to the canoe events at the Olympics (a 20-year campaign that finally came to fruition at the Tokyo Olympics). Together we make up The True Athlete Project, a non-profit based in the United Kingdom and the United States, with a vision of a more compassionate world, achieved through leveraging the transformative power of sport.

The True Athlete Project

In 2014 at the Muhammad Ali Center in Louisville, United States, The True Athlete Project (TAP) was born. After a promising career in Division I college tennis was brought crashing down by four years of desperately poor health and numerous surgeries, TAP's CEO and founder, Sam Parfitt, realised that he had to find a different way of making an impact in the world. His undergraduate research began to focus on the historic use of sport to affect society, and he worked extensively with at-risk Hispanic immigrant youth through soccer. He was introduced to mindfulness and meditation and began to work closely with a leading US sport psychologist. His first job out of college was as the athletic director of a school which had up until then not had a physical education programme. It was an opportunity for Sam to bring to life some of the ideas he had around a new way of teaching and developing young athletes. The programme he initiated involved activities such as parkour, mindfulness, sports poetry and projects on sporting idols such as Muhammad Ali.

The Muhammad Ali Center asked Sam to present his pioneering curriculum at their annual Forum on Athletes and Social Change. While listening to the other presenters talking about using sport to build a better world, Sam felt an overwhelming sense of inspiration to be part of the change. But he also noticed that something was missing – the athletes themselves. It was as if the athletes were left to focus entirely on improving their game, while others got on with the business of harnessing sport's power for social good. But those same athletes are the ones who are most passionate, most committed and with the greatest untapped power, stemming from being natural role models with platforms from which to make their voice heard.

What Sam recognised back then in 2014 was that striving to be the best possible athlete and wanting to make the world a better place could, and indeed should, go hand in hand – a symbiotic relationship.

At that forum Sam, a super-connector, began bringing together a unique group of people to create a vision for harnessing the power of performance sport to bring about positive change in the world. The idea for the True Athlete Project was born with Sam at the helm and an original team that included athletes, coaches, sport and clinical psychologists, mindfulness teachers, policy makers and others with a passionate interest in sport and an unwavering optimism for the future.

The aim was to create something both inspiring and practical, which pointed towards a better future and also showed the path to get there, and which supported those at the heart of sport – athletes, coaches, clubs and federations – in being the drivers of the change that is so needed.

TAP's vision was of sport as a powerful catalyst for a more compassionate world. To achieve that they proposed the following:

- To reimagine sport as a training ground for compassion, mindfulness and mental well-being; and
- To reimagine the athlete as someone who trains mind and body in order to help themselves and others and make the world a better place.

These paradigm shifts would be achieved by designing and delivering a range of pioneering, mindfulness-based programmes at all levels of sport – programmes that prioritise personal growth and an increased awareness in all aspects of life. They would help coaches and organisations skilfully nurture the holistic development of each and every one of their athletes, and enhance each athlete's experience of sport, improving their overall health and performance, and instilling in them a passion for making a positive difference in the world.

At the heart of all these programmes is a philosophy which the TAP team live and breathe through their work and in their daily lives. This book will attempt to describe and define this philosophy.

I have personally seen the immense positive effects that can come from the approaches described in this book – as an athlete myself, in my work with both youth and elite competitors as well as coaches, through The True Athlete Project, and also in my professional role as performance director of the Danish Fencing Federation. The contents of this book are therefore not merely theories but have been shown to be impactful in practice, across a wide spectrum of sports, countries and settings. Where relevant, I give examples of these approaches in action, both from my own experience and that of others. My hope is that the messages in this book, combined with real-life examples and stories, will lead those who are currently on their athletic journey to have a more positive experience than those who went before and for them in turn to help others.

Specifically, this book aims to achieve four things:

- Challenge the current win-at-all-costs culture of elite sport;
- Persuade athletes to think more deeply about the meaning and value of sport;
- Help athletes achieve more of their athletic potential; and
- Give athletes a foundation for enhanced well-being as they go through their sporting career.

These aims are woven throughout the entire book, and in many places come into play simultaneously. Now that you know what we hope you will get out of reading it, let's get started.

PART 1

INTRODUCING THE TRUE
ATHLETE PHILOSOPHY

1   What Is the True Athlete Philosophy and Why Is It Important?

The Burning Platform for Drastic Change in Sport

> *I saw first-hand the power of our example exerted on the hearts and minds of people around the world. But with that came a corollary lesson: an awareness of what we risked when our actions failed to live up to our image and our ideals, the anger and resentment this could breed, the damage that was done.*
>
> — BARACK OBAMA, A PROMISED LAND

Sport *could* be an unequivocally positive force for physical and mental health, creating moments of flow and exhilaration and instilling a joy of life-long learning. It *could* benefit communities and society in general. It *could* bridge social divides and bring people from every walk of life together under a universal language. It *could* provide inspirational role models for everyone. The Olympic Charter points emphatically to this vision for sport:

> *Olympism is a philosophy of life, exalting and combining in a balanced whole the qualities of body, will and mind. Blending sport with culture and education, Olympism seeks to create a way of life based on the joy of effort, the educational value of*

good example, social responsibility and respect for universal fundamental ethical principles.

However, the reality looks depressingly different.

Sport at all levels is rife with unwanted and destructive side-effects, including stress, anxiety, depression, burn-out, bullying, discrimination and corruption, to name just a few. Sport has not come close to delivering on its potential for making the world a better place, neither for those involved nor for society as a whole. From grassroots all the way up to the Olympic and Paralympic level, there are valid concerns with how sport is organised and how athletes are trained and treated.

Jules Boykoff, a former US national soccer player, professor of political science at Pacific University and author of *Power Games: A Political History of the Olympics*, puts it starkly:

In recent years, elite sport has morphed into a vortex of corruption, a regime of enrichment for the already affluent. All too often, human rights and fairness take a backseat to exploitation and inequity. Healthy competition has become hyper-competition. Rosy legacies for sports mega-events have become cagey ways for the rich to pad their bank accounts. Trickle-up economics has colonized the sports world. We can – and must – do better.

The experience of sport at the individual level is often strewn with dispiriting or damaging moments and events. Sport is de-prioritised by the education system, leading to limited options, poor facilities and sub-standard teacher training and support. Increasingly serious competition at youth levels incentivises the treatment and training of children as if they were small adults. This sporting landscape has led to a truly worrying trend of children dropping out of sport in their early teens, never to start again. According to the National Alliance for Youth Sport, of the 40 million children who participate in organised sport in the United States, 70 per cent will drop out by the time they turn 13. As part of the same survey the most common reason given by kids giving up is 'it's just not fun anymore'. In the UK, in 2019, more than half of children and young people were not getting the recommended 60 minutes of physical activity per day, according to Sport England's *Active Lives Children and Young People Survey*.

Considering the untold benefits – physical, mental, social, societal – that are potentially on offer from a lifetime engagement in sport, we should be desperately looking for ways to ensure that sport stays fun throughout children's formative years and beyond. What constitutes 'fun' changes as a person gets older, but we have all the knowledge we need of how to motivate and inspire people of different ages. One such example of our current understanding in this area is Self-Determination Theory, the brainchild of psychologists Edward Deci and Richard Ryan, which proposes that an individual's motivation is highest when the conditions support their experience of competence, autonomy and sense of connection to others. It is a travesty that our sport and education systems are lagging so far behind, providing the polar opposite experiences to participants.

At the elite level, there is a growing body of evidence of the harmful cultures that masquerade as high-performance environments, with national and international organisations around the globe having been shown to foster or cover up the physical, psychological, emotional or sexual abuse of athletes. The scandals that were unveiled in both the United States and Great Britain (GB) Gymnastics federations – with streams of current and former athletes speaking out about the mental, physical and sexual abuse they suffered at the hands of coaches and officials, abuse which was often then dismissed or covered up by those in positions of power – being just two of a long line of abhorrent revelations. A lawsuit filed by 17 former gymnasts in the UK in 2021 claimed widespread physical and mental abuse by British Gymnastics coaches on athletes as young as six years old in a system which prioritised 'podiums over people', according to 2012 Olympian Jennifer Pinches, who spearheaded the complaint. A letter sent before legal action to the governing body alleged, 'British Gymnastics implemented a model of suspended pre-pubescence leading to generations of girls with eating disorders, body image issues, and deliberately stunted physical development'. Simultaneously in 2021 an independent report criticised the Swiss Gymnastics Federation as having a 'totally dysfunctional high-level sports concept' following accusations of systemic humiliation and abuse of their rhythmic gymnasts.

Even the less systematic versions of these toxic high-performance cultures still uphold dehumanising systems which value results over the mental and physical health of the people within the system. In 2020, Choi Suk-hyeon, a 22-year-old South Korean triathlete, took her own life after her complaints of enduring years of physical and mental abuse by coaching staff were ignored by the sporting authorities. In her journal, Suk-hyeon wrote of how she 'shed tears every day' and that she would 'rather die' after repeatedly being 'beaten like a dog'.

Public trust in the integrity of sport at all levels is waning, with trust in the value of elite sport being severely tested by dismaying stories and unethical behaviours. In 2017 a survey of 2,000 British people found that over a third of them declared that their trust in the sporting industry had declined over the previous 12 months, while two-thirds believed that there is a 'widespread problem of ethics in sporting bodies'.

Tales of corruption and unethical behaviour within the highest levels of sports administration are so prevalent as to be almost expected. There are enough examples to fill a book on their own, so let it suffice to mention the most brazen of all followed by the most recent at the time of writing.

The systematic and state-sponsored doping regime of Russian athletes culminated at the Sochi 2018 Winter Olympics. The Russian government had orchestrated a method to switch out the urine samples of known doped athletes for clean substitute urine – via a hole in the doping test lab, no less. The whole, incredible story is captivatingly told in the award-winning documentary *Icarus* by Brian Fogel. Despite overwhelming evidence, including the detailed testimony of the scientist who masterminded the whole debacle, the Russian government is yet to comply with the demand of the World Anti-Doping Association and admit their guilt.

In 2021 an External Review Commission (ERC) into allegations about the International Biathlon Union (IBU) uncovered 'Evidence of systematic corruption and unethical conduct for a decade'. After a two-year investigation, the ERC released a report detailing that the governing body's former president Anders Besseberg had 'no regard for ethical values and no real interest in protecting the sport from cheating'. The report followed criminal investigations into doping, fraud and corruption against Besseberg and IBU's Secretary General, Nicole Resch, and labelled Besseberg's commitment to clean sport as a 'charade', accusing him and his allies of having done 'the absolute minimum that was necessary to preserve a veneer of respectability for the sport'.

There have recently been high-profile cases involving poor athlete physical or mental health stemming from their commodification. In 2017 the *Journals of the American Medical Association Network* (*JAMA*) studied the autopsied brains of 202 American football players who played at different levels of the game. Disturbingly they diagnosed nearly 90 per cent of the brains with chronic traumatic encephalopathy (CTE), a progressive and fatal brain disease which is associated with repeated concussions and blows to the head and is linked to dementia. They also found that the longer the person had played football, the more severe the damage, with 99 per cent of NFL players having CTE. For years the NFL denied any risk posed to the players by these types of injuries, calling concussions 'minor injuries' and stating that there were no long-term health risks associated with them. At the highest level of Britain's equivalent sport, rugby, it has been exposed just how many of the professional players are suffering from mental health issues. The Rugby Players Association (RPA) conducted an anonymous survey in 2018 in which they discovered that 62 per cent of players suffered from some form of mental illness within two years of retiring and that 10 per cent of current players phone the RPA's hotline every year to discuss mental health concerns.

Sports mega-events provide a consistent source of unethical behaviour and objectionable practices. Immense costs and excessive demands are heaped on the host communities, who receive little to none of the promised benefits in return. To prepare for the 2022 Football World Cup in Qatar, 2 million migrant workers have been involved in building the necessary infrastructure. Amnesty International has shown that Qatar's system of sponsorship-based employment traps migrant workers in a cycle of abuse. Workers are prevented from changing jobs or leaving the country by their employers. Late and non-payment of wages, barriers to obtaining justice when rights are violated and the failure to enforce labour laws and penalise employers who abuse their workers are just some of the unethical features of this system.

The 2016 Rio Olympics was plagued with accusations of unethical actions. The illegal displacement of residents, an uptick in police and army violence, the corrupt transfer of public resources into private hands and reneging on environmental promises were among the violations compiled by Children Win in a dossier titled 'Rio 2016 Olympics: The Exclusion Games'. The cost of hosting the Rio Olympics was another scandal, ending up costing just over $13 billion, over a third more than the original budget, at a time of national economic crisis in Brazil. Similar human rights violations and economic concerns have been raised in conjunction with previous Games in Athens, Beijing and London.

This gloomy landscape points to the fact that sport has lost track of its true meaning and lost touch with its core, humanitarian values. Sportsmanship, fair-play and honour have been demoted in importance, both on the field of play and at the organisational level, by a win-at-all-cost attitude. As an athlete, you may experience this through alarmingly packed schedules, the inappropriate behaviour of hyper-competitive parents, stressful or toxic performance environments, a lack of emotional support or perhaps through your own doubts about the integrity of the system you are dedicating your life to.

The driving force is often a cynical business-model approach where the bottom line is results (which can be translated into financial gain), and we have been quick to justify or excuse almost any means to that end. The old excuse 'but they won' should no longer justify an increasingly damaging system.

We must find a way through the fog to bring sport closer to that vision depicted in the Olympic charter. With the joy of participation and deep engagement in physical endeavour, the out-of-body experiences that are accessible to all, the magical, historic moments that inspire those that witness them and can connect us to our parents and their parents, sport can transcend time and culture to bring us closer together and further as a species. But it is clear that we must take active steps to move in this transformative direction and away from the current, bleak trajectory. In the words of Canadian Olympic rower-turned-coach and business consultant Jason Dorland:

> *Sport can choose to maintain the status quo that says competition is a battlefield where combatants use any means possible to destroy one another in the pursuit of winning. Or, it can choose something more meaningful. Therein lies the truest opportunity for sport.*

What is needed is an approach that journeys deeper than the ego-driven realm of wins, losses, medals and the superiority of nations. We need a unified, guiding philosophy that puts athletes, coaches, teams and all those that support them back in touch with the core benefits and true purpose of sport.

This guiding philosophy would light the way for athletes to excel at their sport *and also* become exemplary family members, friends and citizens who have trained mind and body to better nourish their social circle and contribute to their community and ultimately to society as a whole.

Now imagine a world of these *True Athletes*:

- Showing that it is possible to live a life of purpose, separate from material gains
- Who role model positive human connection even while engaged in fierce competition
- Who take care of themselves and the world around them, and create an ongoing ripple effect on their families, friends and community at large

Imagine how society could benefit from generations of these more rounded, socially conscientious and compassionate citizens and role models.

That is a vision which shows how sport could live closer to its ideals. It is also a vision shared by many top athletes who are dismayed to see the potential of sport diminished in front of their eyes. Michael Bennett, the NFL defensive linesman who won the Superbowl with the Seattle Seahawks, puts it vividly:

> *The essence of sport is beautiful. People coming together to achieve a goal regardless of their color, race or religion. Everything about that sounds beautiful. It sounds like a healthy marriage. It sounds like commitment. It sounds like dedication. It sounds like Passion. It sounds like everything worth rising out of bed for. But it gets destroyed by society, by valuing wealth over play; by professionalizing sports for our kids, which sets them against each other even when they are on the same team; by having locker rooms where people can't be themselves; by caring more about winning than the process of how you get there; the glorification of those kinds of values is what makes sport toxic. I believe that sport has a role in changing society, from youth leagues to the pros.*

Introducing the True Athlete Philosophy

> *Plants thrive under particular conditions, and biologists can now tell us how sunlight and water get converted into plant growth. People thrive under particular conditions, and psychologists can now tell us how love and work get converted into happiness and a sense of meaning.*
>
> — JONATHAN HAIDT

The main objective of the True Athlete Philosophical approach is to address the loss of meaning and diminished values inherent to the current hyper-results-focused approach in sport. What we are offering up here is a paradigm shift, a new foundation from which we can begin to unleash sport's true potential.

The True Athlete Philosophy is a framework of guiding principles and practices aimed at athletes and those around them who wish to get much more from their time in sport than medals and accolades: to highlight how sport can prepare you wonderfully for life in general. It is a structure around which you can build up your own personal philosophy, using those elements that you find most relevant and valuable. It draws on a range of thinking across sport, clinical and positive psychology, the philosophies of the Eastern-originating martial arts, and as far back as the ancient philosophies, most notably Stoicism and Buddhism.

Stoicism is a practical philosophy for life from the ancient Roman and Greek era, based on a logical view of the world and our place in it. Stoicism teaches that accepting the world as it is, living with virtue and treating each other fairly is the route to happiness and meaning in life.

Buddhism originated in India between the 6th and 4th centuries BC. There is no god in Buddhism; and it has been described by some as a spiritual tradition rather than an organised religion. Buddhism promotes meditation as a path to greater awareness, compassion and wisdom, and provides the path to follow that can lead to achieving the ultimate goal of Buddhist spiritual life – to alleviate the suffering of all beings.

From these fonts of knowledge and wisdom, combined with the work, research and lived experience of the True Athlete Project team we slowly homed in on the most relevant underlying principles that would lead to a meaningful, thriving experience within sport. Furthermore, as well as having a direct health and well-being objective, we highlight these principles for their capacity to contribute to improving performance.

The True Athlete Philosophy is designed to replace the win-at-all-cost model and offers a compelling pathway to genuine, sustainable high performance.

We lay the foundations of the Philosophy in this chapter by exploring the practical value of having a philosophy and then by addressing the big picture: what is the purpose of sport? Then in Part 2 we explore that purpose by describing in greater detail, and a more practical sense, how we might better go about achieving it. To that aim we point to certain virtues that a True Athlete aspires to uphold. We promote these specific virtues as being critical to the mission of unleashing more of sport's potential, but they are certainly not the whole picture. Every human being will inhabit and exhibit a wide range of character traits, and all hold their own distinct value.

Part 3 is where the rubber meets the road. We provide a practical guide to some of the mental and emotional approaches and practices that will help you train and develop as a True Athlete. As with improving any skill, it takes time and commitment to develop the traits and embody the values that you most want to define you and your life. Some of the elements of Part 3 describe non-traditional perspectives and some are daily practices that can be built into your very own True Athlete training programme. All the elements in the chapters of Part 3 can enhance performance but are equally valuable in working towards a healthy, happy life alongside sport.

What Use Is a Philosophical Framework?

The body and its parts are a river, the soul a dream and mist, life is warfare and a journey far from home, lasting reputation is oblivion. Then what can guide us? Only philosophy.
— MARCUS AURELIUS, 'THE PHILOSOPHER KING'

A philosophy is our way of creating meaning from what we see in the world, which in turn governs how we act and interact in it.

Your philosophy can have a profound effect on all aspects of your life, including your approach to sport. It is a lens through which you see the world, and which distorts or colours everything you perceive accordingly. It will influence every choice and decision you make along your way, including

- Your choice of club or team
- Your approach to training
- Who you choose to surround yourself with and how you relate to those people
- Your responses to challenges and opportunity
- The character you display in both good and bad times
- How long you remain engaged in your sport and the durability of your passion for it

It is therefore of utmost importance to have consciously explored and developed your own philosophy.

A well-chosen philosophy can be a powerful and stable source of inspiration and motivation, as it gives a deeper sense of meaning and purpose that is not affected by the ever-changing winds of sport and life. A career in sport is inevitably turbulent, full of highs and lows – including not only exuberant wins, close friendships and moments of intense bonding but also harsh losses, injuries, performance dips and broken relationships, to name a few. It therefore makes sense to cultivate an approach that finds motivation and inspiration wholly independent of the more superficial measures of success.

John Wooden, an American basketball coach, won 10 NCAA titles in 12 years with UCLA, including an unmatched 7 in a row. He is often referred to as *the greatest coach of all time*, both for his record on the court and also for his detailed philosophy, focused heavily on character development. He introduced his definition of what really matters in sport at the very start of his coaching career, and it never changed afterwards:

> *Success is peace of mind which is a direct result of self-satisfaction in knowing that you made the effort to become the best of which you are capable.*

Every athlete has a philosophical approach to their sport. Some will be better thought-through than others, with a greater degree of conscious design. Certainly, some are not grounded in those principles that lead along a positive, healthy and motivated path towards long-term well-being and fulfilment. Consider, for example, the athlete who believes that a cut-throat and self-centred approach is the only way to the top. They may well find that this approach can get them all the glory they seek, but they will have burnt all their bridges along the way, perhaps earning plenty of respect for their skills, but none for their character. They will find at the end of it all that achieving the peak they were clambering towards gives them no lasting satisfaction. They are doomed to become a bereft champion: nobody's role model.

American psychologist and professor at the University of California at Davis, Robert Emmons, suggested that most of people's life goals can be sorted into four categories:

- Work and achievement
- Relationships and intimacy
- Religion and spirituality
- Self-transcendence and generativity (which is defined as leaving a legacy, contributing to society and transcending self-interest)

Emmons found that although it is generally good for you to pursue goals, not all goals are equally likely to contribute to well-being. People who strive primarily for achievement and wealth are less happy, on average, than those whose goals focus on the other three categories. Similarly, different life philosophies are not all equally likely to contribute to well-being and a sense of purpose and meaning.

Perhaps the most common philosophy of today's sports teams and individual athletes, one which is overtly cultivated by modern culture, is that winning is all-important and glory attained is worth almost any cost. This type of philosophy has been evident in the shocking revelations of systemic abuse in both US and British gymnastics – a culture of fear, humiliation and disregard for athlete welfare which led the British Rio Olympics bronze medallist artistic gymnast Amy Tinkler to say in an interview with ITV news – 'I would give up that medal to not have gone through what I did'.

This philosophy is at the heart of the crisis of sport. It is an ego-driven approach entirely at odds with what we know from philosophy, religion and psychology about how to lead a mentally and emotionally healthy and productive life that is meaningful. It is not even necessarily the best approach to winning, and we will show you why, later in this book.

One thought leader in this space, Cath Bishop, wrote *The Long Win – The Search for a Better Way to Succeed*, which details how modern society's obsession with winning has gotten out of hand and the many ways that this approach is misguided and damaging. Bishop has a CV worthy of multiple lifetimes and is brimming with authority on what success in life looks like – three-time British Olympic rower, with a silver medal from the Athens 2004 Olympics; conflict-zone diplomat with the UK Foreign Office, with placements in Iraq and Bosnia; executive and leadership coach working with teams and leaders across business, sport and education. In the book, Bishop writes, 'Simple, narrow definitions of what winning means can lead to serious unforeseen consequences. The dichotomous "winning is good, losing is bad" view doesn't hold up to the scrutiny of real life. In fact, that mentality is not serving us well at all.'

She goes on to explain a healthier and more helpful approach to success – what she calls Long Win Thinking. It is, in itself, a type of life philosophy, centred on three key areas which contribute to living your best life, full of meaning – Clarity, Constant Learning and Connection.

Just as Bishop's book highlights, it should be society's collective duty to try to shed light on how different philosophies impact us and our lives, to adjust those that are either harmful or not fit for purpose, and to provide a framework for creating a more healthy, rational and meaningful lens for viewing the world.

A fresh, more appropriate philosophy will provide a form of road map for how you, the athlete, can gain the absolute most from your time in sport, that goes beyond simply the results or level that you achieve. This is especially relevant given the percentage of athletes who either are put off by their early experiences in sport or drop out long before they achieve their vision of success. It would provide you with our best understanding of how to live a healthy, meaningful life based on maximising the unique environments, opportunities and challenges within sport. There is an unparalleled opportunity for you as an athlete to create a life of purpose and well-being by incorporating effective practices and habits into your daily life. This represents an integral journey you will undertake alongside your training and performance that will act as a powerful, stable protection against the stress, anxiety, burn-out and drop-out that afflicts so many young athletes.

There is also great potential in drawing athletes of all backgrounds together in pursuit of a common, higher purpose. This connection with many others who are engaged on the same pilgrimage can provide the individual athlete with a deep sense of belonging, and participation in a broader mission than simply their own search for improved performance.

If you are an athlete or a coach, hopefully you will be inspired to use this book as a starting point for creating your own personal philosophy, based on what you value most about yourself, the experiences you want in sport and the impact you want to have in the world.

The Wider Implications of a Shared Philosophical Approach

The broad adoption of a guiding philosophy for sport such as this one has numerous practical benefits that would reach across the full spectrum of sport culture, from global institutions to national federations, sports clubs, schools, right down to the individual athletes, coaches and fans. This is due to the scope of the framework, which incorporates both idealism and realism – from an expansive, soaring purpose of sport to a set of ground-level practices and strategies that an individual may implement and benefit from directly.

Philosophy, with its unique power to draw out meaning and assert value, can help lead sport into a bold new era. In order to be successful, this philosophy must be grand in its ambition and broad in its implications in order to counteract the most pernicious aspects of sport culture so that it may once again stand for something truly aspirational in the eyes of the world.

A higher purpose can align motivations across disciplines and borders and provide a shared standard that all organisations and leaders may be guided, uplifted and aligned by. The clarity that comes with a commonly shared vision allows us to commit more fully. The inherent inspiration that comes from having ambitious goals means that we will reach further.

This can become a powerful connector for organisations with their stakeholders. If they can honestly show that their actions follow a truer path, then the mission they are undertaking can be universally lauded. As Simon Sinek puts it so eloquently in his 2009 TED talk, 'How Great Leaders Inspire Action': 'People don't buy what you do; they buy why you do it, and what you do simply serves as the proof of what you believe.'

There will follow a paradigm shift in sport – no longer to be focused solely on talent and performance but enhanced to include greater awareness of the practices and culture that encourage people's inherent goodness and kindness to shine through – to reinvent sport as an unmatched vehicle for bringing people together in mutual understanding and respect.

Higher Purpose of Sport

*To sustain and guide you, nourish a triple will: the will to the physical joy which results from intense muscular effort – even excessive and violent effort – next the will to honest, complete and unremitting altruism ... **for mark well the coming society will be altruistic or will be nothing** (my emphasis). Choose between that and chaos. Lastly the will to understand things as a whole.*

— Pierre de Coubertin

In this Philosophy the higher purpose of sport is:

To create a more compassionate, vibrant and peaceful world.

The value proposition of sport has always been prodigious. From Olympism to the many Eastern martial arts that have founding philosophies, there is a common thread of conviction that the purpose of sport should be no less than the betterment of society as a whole.

The philosophy of the Korean martial art Tae Kwon Do is to build a more peaceful world through the development of the character, personality and moral and ethical principles of each practitioner. Aikido, a more modern Japanese martial art, was developed by Morihei Ueshiba as a way to combine martial practice, philosophy and religious beliefs. Aikido can be translated as 'way of the harmonious spirit'; and it aims to better people's lives, make their spirit blossom and help them become strong by making better people and a better world. Similarly, Jigoro Kano, the founder of Judo, said: 'Judo is the way to the most effective use of both physical and spiritual strength. By training you in attacks and defenses it refines your body and your soul and helps you make the spiritual essence of judo a part of your very being. In this way you are able to perfect yourself and contribute something of value to the world. This is final goal of judo discipline.'

There is every reason to agree with these well-established philosophies. Sport is a response to life; and within sport and competition we find the fullest expression of the human spirit, including euphoric highs and debilitating lows, never-ending challenges, failures, stories of heroic, seemingly impossible physical and mental feats and everything in-between. There is good reason, then, to argue that such a training ground should aim for the loftiest of goals. After all, sport is unmatched in its capacity for shaping lives and has been ubiquitous across all human cultures from the dawn of civilisation. Sadly, these types of founding philosophies are entirely missing from modern sports. Without such an anchor, those sports are more susceptible to drifting far from the noble principles of sport itself.

However, the guiding principles of sport in general have not been constant throughout history, or across cultures. Sport has long been used as a tool to achieve specific social goals. At different times in history sport has been an apparatus for training soldiers fit for war, building an industrialised workforce and in its current manifestation as a proxy for nationalism and the comparative power of nation-states. The nations close to the top of the Olympic medal table spend vast sums to support their Olympic hopeful athletes in the four-year period between the Games. This is the competitive grandstanding equivalent of the space race between the United States and USSR in the 1950s and 1960s.

Sport has also been used by different cultures to achieve varied purposes, with a range of underlying principles. The modern sport of lacrosse has its origins in stick and ball games played by various Native American communities. One such variant, 'Tewaaraton', meaning 'little brother of war' in the Mohawk language, was played by anywhere between 100 and 1,000 men from opposing tribes on vast open plains between villages. The purpose of the game was not only to toughen up young men to become warriors but also for recreational and religious reasons. Similarly, Australian Football is generally thought to have derived from an Aboriginal ritual practice 'Marngrook', which translates from the language of the Gunditjmara people as 'Game ball'. Marngrook was not only a way of keeping people fit and healthy but also a highly social activity that strengthens family and social connections. Much like today's sporting landscape, Marngrook teams would travel to play against different communities, forging relationships and connections further from home.

The associated values of sport are also highly variable. The world watched as Diego Maradona used his hand – the famous 'Hand of God' incident – to score a goal against England in the quarter-final of the 1986 World Cup. He followed that up, just minutes later, with what came to be known as the 'Goal of the Century'. Argentina won the match 2-1 and went on to win the entire tournament, solidifying Maradona's status as one of the greatest players in history. While the English saw the hand-ball goal as a travesty against sportsmanship and a moral failure on the part of Maradona, the Argentines viewed it altogether differently – a perspective rooted in the concept of 'Viveza Criolla'. *Viveza criolla*, specific to that region of South America, describes a kind of cleverness and cunning determination to defy authority and circumvent the rules, and doing so sneakily and successfully. This attitude relates back to the struggles of the working class to redress the balance against the rich, who had successfully rigged the system to their own advantage. That quarter-final between England and Argentina took place just four years after the British had utterly dominated the Argentines in the highly mismatched Falklands War. To Maradona and his countrymen then, the British were the colonial power, and anything would go to put one over them. Asif Kapadia, the documentarian who made a film about Maradona's life, sums it up: 'How do you hurt the colonial power? You cheat. You do it such a way that it hurts more …. And that's why they love him, because he did the two things – the genius and the cheat – three minutes apart, against England.'

For Argentinians, this streetwise approach is an inherent part of their national game – football being for them a traditionally working-class sport and akin to a religion. This contributes to the idea that there is no universality to sport. It can be utilised, viewed and played in a multitude of ways.

Some will argue that elite sport is first and foremost entertainment, and that it should be treated as such. Such is the premise that professional wrestling has adopted with great success. Or else they believe sport is a business, albeit a less transactional kind of business where the 'customers' build a strong emotional relationship to the 'product' being sold. While professional sport is a business in many respects, and elite sport is often highly entertaining, these labels thoroughly diminish what could be achieved through sport. It is vital that we do not become limited by what elite sport has been in the past. The question we must ask is: What does society need from sport now?

Our answer to this question is as follows: The purpose of sport should be to address the existential crises and social injustices that are prevalent today. We should harness the power of this intensely collaborative drive for excellence, and use it to nurture generations of highly compassionate, self-aware and responsible citizens. These citizens will, in turn, lend their voice and their power to help our species overcome struggles and progress.

Therefore, the highest goal of sport should be the betterment of individuals and society, based on a foundation of love and respect for self, others and our natural environment, for the differences between people and their opinions and attitudes to life, and ultimately acknowledging the far greater commonality between all people, striving to achieve happiness and avoid suffering.

According to the 14th Dalai Lama, inter-dependence is a fundamental law of nature, which is the reason humans cherish *love and compassion* above all else, as they bring the greatest tranquillity and happiness. Regardless of how capable, energetic and creative we are as individuals, we rely on each other and on a thriving natural habitat for our health, happiness and ultimate survival. This fact leads inextricably to our shared responsibility for our fellow humans and the planet we call home, which, if embraced, brings a powerful sense of well-being, contentment and purpose.

The ultimate aim for our species should be unbounded love and compassion; and although it is unobtainable in any practical sense, it can give us a direction of travel. The vibrancy in the higher purpose statement is born of a society developed with the flourishing and interconnectivity of its citizens as its foundation. The term encapsulates the buzzing energy, creativity and drive that would arise within such a society.

This higher purpose is to be achieved through the development of *True Athletes*.

While this book focuses mainly on the individual athlete's approach to sport, an essential aspect of the higher purpose described here is that it takes a whole village to nurture a True Athlete. There is important work to be done by coaches, parents, teams, clubs and governing bodies in supporting every athlete and creating the environments and cultures that provide healthy, meaningful experiences based on long-term principles rather than short-term victories. We challenge anyone reading this who supports athletes on their journey to consider what it would require of themselves and the environment they create if they embraced this higher purpose.

Definition of a True Athlete

To be a well-rounded person and know what's going on in the world around you, to have a perspective outside of your sport, is important for every athlete.

— VENUS WILLIAMS

What is described here is an idealistic vision of the True Athlete. It is not practical to imagine that any one person could live up to every quality of this vision. So, when you read through this definition, and indeed the rest of the book, please don't get caught thinking that you need to live up to every bit of it. In reality a True Athlete is anyone who aspires to this vision and this Philosophy, all the while acknowledging that there is no perfection to obtain here, but just a continuous process of working with themselves in order to achieve more of their potential and be of greater value to their community. Much like training any physical quality, your character traits and living according to certain values can also be trained, through attention and discipline.

A True Athlete has

Perspective – They train mind and body in order to know themselves better, help others and make a positive contribution to the world.

Self-awareness – They are mindful of the elements of character, behaviour and thought that lead one towards a healthy life of meaning.

Emotional control – They have awareness of, and control within, the space between an event and their response to that event and are skilful in choosing how they react, rather than subject to automatic responses.

Inner stability – They have a character with a stable yet flexible structure (integrity) to withstand all storms.

Grace – They have stable foundations and firm, though not rigid, boundaries which allow for great acts of compassion and selflessness. (A True Athlete knows they have the internal resources to spare for this purpose, and that this is the route to fulfilling their responsibility.)

Humanity – They embrace their vulnerabilities and imperfections without judgement.

Love – They have love for themselves and others.

Consideration for others – They have gratitude and respect for teammates, opponents, officials and others.

Social conscience – They are keenly aware of the platform they have and of their responsibility to make a positive contribution that comes with it.

Curiosity – They are a scholar of their sport, exploring the context in which they operate.

Next up, in Part 2, we will dive into four virtues that underpin this depiction of a True Athlete and that flesh out the True Athlete Philosophy.

Chapter Summary

- Sport is not coming close to fulfilling its potential for doing good in the world – from kids sport all the way up to Olympic level there is a damaging disconnect with the essential values of sport.
- What is needed is a strong guiding philosophy that underpins sport at all levels and which moves away from the win-at-all-costs approach that is currently so dominant.
- The True Athlete Philosophy combines ancient wisdom and current knowledge to propose an approach to competitive sport which is healthier and can unleash more of each athlete's potential.
- Throughout history sport has been utilised to meet the specific needs of society. It is time to define a higher purpose of sport which addresses humanity's current urgent needs.
- Our proposed higher purpose – *To create a more compassionate, vibrant and peaceful world* – is to be achieved through the development of True Athletes.
- True Athletes are well-rounded, compassionate and socially conscientious citizens and role models.

PART 2

THE VIRTUES OF THE TRUE ATHLETE PHILOSOPHY

2 Treat Yourself and Others with Compassion

People become house builders by building houses, harp players through playing the harp. We grow to be just by doing things which are just.

— ARISTOTLE

Introducing the Virtues

The counterpoint we propose to the win-at-all-costs approach with its unintended, yet damaging, side-effects is to advance sport as a widely recognised, uniquely respected vehicle for individual character development.

There are many traditional traits associated with being an athlete which are also of great benefit for life beyond sport. Here, these are called *the traditional athlete traits*. These traditional traits are, for the most part, essential for making it to the elite levels of your sport.

Examples of traditional athlete traits include:

- Discipline
- Excellence
- Hard work
- Adaptability
- Commitment

- Respect
- Teamwork

However, what is being revealed to us now is that these traditional athletic traits simply do not provide enough of a foundation for becoming a well-rounded individual with good mental health and living a life of purpose and meaning. We have seen time and time again that some of the very best athletes – hall of famers, record breakers, Olympic gold medal winners – have reached the pinnacle of their sporting careers only to realise that they still feel unfulfilled, that something is missing. The best of the best can also struggle with mental health issues such as depression and identity crises.

Dame Kelly Holmes is one of the superstars of British Olympic sport. Her career culminated in a sensational double gold in the 800 m and 1,500 m at the 2004 Athens Olympics, rocketing her to stardom in her home country. But just prior to that event Holmes found herself in a very dark state of mind. At the age of 27 she was already an Olympic medallist, with a bronze in Sydney 2000, when a series of injuries and illnesses sent her spiralling into depression. Speaking about how she felt in 2003, right before her career defining success, she said:

I just looked in the mirror and hated myself. I wanted the floor to open up, I wanted to jump in that space, I wanted it to close and I didn't want to go back out. I was in such a bad way. Then I started cutting myself.

There is no doubt that Holmes had developed herself to the peak of human potential in some areas, which made it possible for her to reach so far in her sport. But there were clearly some aspects of her training *for life* that were missing from her journey.

In order to unleash sport's fullest potential as an unequivocally positive force for good in the world, we must channel more of our attention towards the character traits that will help you, the athlete, truly flourish in life while also helping you excel in your sport. These traits, that we will call here *The True Athlete Virtues*, are those that represent our best wisdom and understanding on how to lead a good, psychologically healthy life of meaning, and which, when properly cultivated, will also directly benefit your sporting performance.

Aristotle taught us that we can gain virtues by practising them in our daily life, and by emulating role models until they become habit and we eventually embody them. In this way virtues are exactly the same as any skill that an athlete improves at. This is a pivotal point, because it highlights the fact that character is not set in stone. The timid person who practices courage regularly enough will become a courageous person. The restless person who practices patience enough will become a more patient person. If you identify a virtue that you want to define who you are and how others perceive you, then look out for those who embody that virtue and seek out ways to practice it as often as possible. We hope that the following virtues can inspire you on that path.

The True Athlete Virtues

- Treat yourself and others with *compassion.*
- Live with *integrity.*
- Acknowledge and embrace *responsibility* for your own journey and that of your community.
- Grow your *awareness* of the present moment and of what truly matters in life.

It is feasible for an athlete to embody very little of these four virtues and still reach the very top of their sport. Carried forward by the traditional athlete traits alone, they can become the most fearsome competitor. However, we believe that such an athlete would find themselves at the end of a prodigious career without any lasting sense of fulfilment, or connection with any deeper meaning. Indeed, there are many examples of such highly rated athletes, who may have brought happiness to many of their fans but alas not to themselves.

Michael Phelps achieved more in the swimming pool than most people could even dream of achieving, becoming the most decorated Olympian of all time, winning 28 medals over 4 Olympics, including 23 gold. Yet even throughout the peaks of his career, Phelps suffered from severe depression. In the documentary 'The Weight of Gold', on the epidemic of mental health issues among world-class athletes, which Phelps co-produced, he said:

> Yeah, I won a s--t-ton of medals. I had a great career. So what? I thought of myself as 'just a swimmer'. Not a human being.

To help avoid this kind of troubling attitude, athletes must be introduced to a broader perspective on what they are engaged in. For many, this could be a key to reaching even higher in their sport. Though in the case of Phelps, it is difficult to imagine he could have achieved more than he has. Embracing a broader perspective could allow athletes to approach their career in a way that elevates them not just as an athlete, but as a person, and that also enriches those around them.

These selected virtues are not entirely distinct from each other. There are many areas in which they merge into, complement or underpin one another, which becomes increasingly evident within many of the practical examples introduced here.

This blurring of the lines between virtues shows that there is a lot of subjectivity; one person can interpret a virtue very differently to another and draw different conclusions and distinctions. This is the case for all such virtues, traits or values. For example, being respectful and being kind have much in common and it would be impossible to draw a line between them that everyone could agree on. Thankfully that level of detailed definition is not important or relevant in this context. The fact that many traits and values are difficult to define and have so much overlap is a sign that there are no absolutes when it comes to moral or ethical behaviour. We can learn to embrace the fact that we cannot hope to become perfectly respectful, or perfectly kind. *Kind* is not a place you can ever arrive at, but rather a direction you can seek to travel in, always checking that you are on the right path. This mindset can be useful for athletes to be able to adopt when their pursuit of perfection is causing undue stress. Instead of a fruitless search for the unobtainable they can switch to the thoroughly accepting, forgiving and essentially human effort of trying to be their best self.

It is important to note two things here. The first is that these virtues are not intended to replace personal values but instead to complement them. There is an equal number of valid paths to the fulfilled life as there are people on earth and even when we agree on certain shared values there are many different approaches to striving to live by them. Secondly, by highlighting these virtues we do not seek to diminish any other virtues, traits or values, many of which have an equally important role in creating a positive and rounded human experience. The purpose of this part of the book is to introduce those virtues that hold special significance in the mission to unleash more of sport's potential power for good in the world, and to highlight some of the key ways in which they uphold this heightened meaning for life and sport.

Treat Yourself and Others with Compassion

Compassion is not religious business, it is human business, it is not luxury, it is essential for our own peace and mental stability, it is essential for human survival.

— THE DALAI LAMA

Athletes all too commonly beat themselves up for making mistakes or after disappointing results; and that in turn takes a psychological toll, potentially affecting future performances. They also tend to be their own worst critics, much harsher on themselves than they would be to a teammate, friend or family member in the same position. Many think that they need to feel this way, that their capacity to criticise themselves is an integral part of why they are successful at their sport. They rationalise that it forces them to work harder because they *hate losing so much* and they can't be satisfied with anything less than perfect. Underneath this rationalisation is the worry that if they didn't feel awful after making mistakes or losing that would mean they didn't care enough to perform well.

I should know having had that exact mindset for much of my early sporting career. I used to take losing deeply to heart. At the same time, I used to almost welcome the pain, because it showed how much I cared and how much I wanted to get better. It would take me ages to fully get over a bad loss. I wore my emotions like a badge to show others that losing was not acceptable to me. My disposition was by no means unusual among my contemporaries. Such a punishing mindset is often accepted and even appreciated in sport culture – the consummate professional athlete, always striving, never satisfied, unaccepting of anything less than perfect. But it is based on a fallacy, and one that damages athletes' well-being and their performances. On top of that it is limiting sport from reaching its true potential in the world.

The power of those negative emotions can motivate, but it is a motivation based on fear and a desire to avoid the inevitable backlash and self-judgement that comes from failure. It distracts from performance far more than it benefits it. If we truly want our athletes to stay focused and calm under pressure, then it doesn't make sense to allow (or even encourage) them to continue beating themselves up when things don't go well.

I was working with one young athlete who was competing in their first youth world championships. They were having a bad day and after one particularly hard loss I had to hold their hands down to stop them literally beating themselves in the head.

Some athletes can train themselves to master that fear and continue on to great achievements and contributions to sport and beyond, but many more will quit or burn out early in their careers because the mental-emotional toll is simply too great. The fact that those athletes do not want to put up with such consistent and negative self-judgement should not mean that they must leave competitive sport for good. Especially when there is a better path to follow that could make for a much healthier relationship between an athlete and their own performance, as well as leading to an improvement in the performance itself.

The basis of the approach we are proposing here is in training self-compassion, which is to be used during the moments of suffering that competitive athletes undoubtedly face. At its heart, self-compassion is about treating yourself with the same kindness that you would a close friend – to be forgiving, understanding and sympathetic and to recognise that inadequacy and making mistakes are things that everyone experiences. It would be like having an inner dialogue that resembles a combination of a kind coach and your closest teammate. They would be endlessly encouraging and forgiving, because they want you to do your best and help you be your best, without suffering needlessly.

Another athlete I worked with struggled with a persistently negative inner dialogue. We made a plan that he should telephone his sister, with whom he had a very close and loving relationship, when he was being particularly tough on himself. Wherever he was competing in the world he would have a talk with her, and it would immediately dampen the worst of his mood. After a while he could start to internalise her warm, forgiving advice, so eventually he didn't need to speak to her every time and could play the compassionate role for himself.

Of course, you don't deserve to suffer simply for missing a shot or losing a match. For many athletes it is easy to play the forgiving teammate role, because deep down they know that is how they will get the best from their teammate, but it becomes much harder to play that role for themselves. This holds true for much of the general population where kindness to friends, family or neighbours is highly valued, but kindness to oneself is perceived as selfish, narcissistic or too soft. Why are we making things harder for ourselves and treating ourselves in ways that we would never treat others?

In the example I gave earlier about the young athlete at the world championships, we had a long talk in the cafeteria after the competition was over, once they had calmed down. We made the agreement that they never deserved to treat themselves like that, regardless of how bad the performance was. They needed to realise (and perhaps also be told by someone) that they were worth more than that.

Self-compassion as a trait has been shown to pay off greatly in terms of psychological well-being, and it is ideally suited to creating a healthier culture of sport while at the same time helping athletes perform better. Ground-breaking compassion researcher Kristin Neff describes self-compassion as being made up of three parts that combine to make for a more balanced, healthy approach to life's struggles. These three parts are:

Self-kindness: Essentially treating ourselves as we would a good friend. Instead of having a critical or disparaging inner dialogue, we offer ourselves warmth and acceptance.

Common humanity: Recognising that making mistakes and being flawed are common to all human beings and are part of the human condition.

Mindfulness: This is about being aware of your experience in the present moment, with balance and without judging what is going on in your mind.

Let's consider these concepts and explore how they relate back to sport.

Self-kindness

Self-kindness has such powerful implications for athletes, but at the same time, it is almost an alien concept to many. It may be one of the most under-rated mental approaches for athletes to adopt. Sport culture teaches all too often that it is good to be hard on yourself, to be self-critical to the extreme until you have reached your goals. What follows from that logic is that self-kindness, forgiveness and acceptance will undermine your motivation to reach your goals. Later we will discuss the myths and misunderstandings around self-compassion, but for now we will point out the glaring reality that seems to be hidden from view to many.

When self-criticism does motivate, it is born from a desire to avoid the harsh self-judgement that follows an unsatisfactory performance, essentially born from fear. But when we fear the consequences of failure, we inhibit our ability to push our limits, take risks and even our willingness to *try* in the first place. Using self-kindness to eliminate those fears gives us motivation simply and powerfully, because we care. We want the best for ourselves, to be our best selves and to do things that will make us happier, better people such as taking on challenges and learning new skills. This is motivation born from *love*.

Research has shown that people who are kinder to themselves have less fear of failure, and when they do fail they are more likely to try again. This makes intuitive sense as self-compassion requires that we be aware of our weaknesses but without attaching judgement. This provides a solid, positive foundation to work to improve on them.

To conceptualise these two different approaches, you can call to mind two different coaches. One is ruthlessly critical when their athlete or team messes up, putting them down and constantly highlighting their failings. The other is the compassionate coach, who reassures their players that it is human to make mistakes, keeps the focus on how they can improve on their weaknesses and gives them the support to work on those goals without fear of reproach. Which coach will get the best out of their players? Which coach will be more likely to keep hold of their athletes for longer? Under which coach are injuries and poor mental health likely to be covered up or hidden? Perhaps most importantly, which coach would you most want to work with?

It is the compassionate coach's voice that we want athletes to incorporate into their inner dialogue, to contribute to a healthier and more stable psychological foundation on which to build. This would also have significant knock-on effects for the culture of sport in general and specifically on the longevity of sports careers, the retention of athletes at all levels as well as their enjoyment of sport, thereby increasing their potential to be positive role models in society.

Common Humanity

We are all flawed in our own ways but when considering our own shortcomings and struggles we often tend to feel isolated while thinking that everyone else is doing just fine. It is much more comforting, logical and accurate to recognise that everyone is in the same boat, and that life's challenges and personal failures are all part of what it means to be human.

Gaining a greater sense of common humanity brings with it a broader perspective which helps to put sports in a more appropriate context. Athletes under pressure can get trapped in a mindset that feels like their whole world hangs in the balance, often described as *catastrophic thinking*. All sport is a game, and though there can be lots of money involved and it is a livelihood for many, it is vitally important, for performance and general well-being, to be able to keep things in a healthy perspective. The idea that *we are all in the same boat, battling the waves of human existence together* is much more comforting and motivating than thinking we are each an island with our own, unique troubles.

Creating more awareness of our common experience can also help athletes develop respect for their teammates and competitors, as well as officials and other sports employees and volunteers. I can testify to the profound improvement in my experience of doing my sport when I came round to this way of thinking.

Mindfulness

Mindfulness is essential to self-compassion because we must first become aware that we are suffering in order to help ourselves. A key part of mindfulness is not to be swept away by our thoughts and emotions but to simply notice them. When we over-identify with a thought or emotion we are not in a balanced place from which to consider how we want to react to it, we are not mindful but instead are caught up in our mind's tumult.

Mindfulness training is particularly effective for creating calm in times of need and for detaching from the power of negative or distracting emotions. It is also increasingly being recognised for its connection to the experience of flow or being in the zone, as both require an all-encompassing focus on the here and now. Thousands of years of experience have shown us very clearly that you can indeed train your brain to be more present and aware, and the implications of this for sport performance, as well as life off the field of play, are enormous.

Elite athletes have practised mindfulness for over 40 years to gain more control over their minds, and therefore their reactions and behaviours during emotionally charged moments. Famously, under the guidance of legendary coach Phil Jackson, both the Chicago Bulls with Michael Jordan and LA Lakers with Kobe Bryant worked with mindfulness teacher George Mumford to help the players with the mental side of their game.

Mindfulness plays a vital role in enhancing self-compassion, and in addition to the benefits outlined above, it will undoubtedly play an increasingly pivotal role in athlete development culture. A more detailed dive into mindfulness comes in Part 3.

Myths and Misconceptions of Self-compassion

You may think this all sounds nice, but that it misses the cutting edge that athletes need to succeed. Or, that self-compassion is clearly a good thing to aim for, but its place is in Buddhist retreats, not elite training camps. Self-compassion is not a well-understood concept in much of the Western world and so it is important to get to grips with what it means to understand the basis of any misconceptions we may have.

As we have seen, self-compassion is being open to, and aware of, one's own suffering with a desire to alleviate that suffering through warmth, forgiveness and kindness. It involves a non-judgemental understanding of one's own pain, mistakes and failures, and helps us see these experiences as a normal part of the human experience.

According to compassion researchers, such as Kristin Neff, Paul Gilbert and Amber Mosewich, among others, high levels of self-compassion are linked with increased feelings of happiness, optimism, curiosity and connectedness, as well as decreased anxiety, depression, rumination and fear of failure.

Harbouring any of the following misconceptions around self-compassion is fully understandable since our current culture of sport has long propagated a directly opposing attitude: that an athlete must suffer after mistakes or losses to show that they truly care, and that coaches must be severe and unforgiving in order to get results. Sport culture does not always openly encourage these perspectives, but it has not done enough to disabuse people of them.

The most common concerns or misconceptions about self-compassion are:

- Self-compassion is soft.
- Self-compassion undermines motivation to work hard and to keep improving.
- Self-compassion is self-indulgent.
- Self-compassion is narcissistic or too self-centred.
- Athletes need self-esteem, not self-compassion.

Self-compassion Is Soft

Increased focus in this area of research, most notably by Neff and her colleagues, has proven that self-compassion helps people cope and be more resilient at emotionally difficult times. A study published in the *Journal of Traumatic Stress* indicates that high scores on a self-compassion scale are linked to lower levels of post-traumatic stress disorder in military veterans. Military veterans, exposed to the toughest of environments, including real-life or death situations, display healthier physiological responses to stress when they have higher levels of self-compassion. Athletes, who experience less intense pressure than military personnel, will benefit from this same healthier response to the stresses they face.

It is not hard to imagine the kind of inner strength and deep resilience that can come from embracing a solid foundation of acceptance and kindness, combined with an understanding that to struggle and fail is an inherent part of the human condition.

Self-compassion Undermines Motivation to Work Hard and to Keep Improving

Motivation derived from a base of self-compassion is at least as effective, far healthier and more sustainable over the long term than a motivation based on self-criticism and dissatisfaction. The self-critical approach to motivation derives its power from a desire to avoid the backlash that comes from failure, essentially from fear of the negative after-effect. Self-compassion takes away that fear and replaces it with a desire to drive towards self-improvement simply because we care about being the best version of ourselves. This is, at its heart, developing a mastery mindset. It is the classic battle of love vs fear; both sides can muster great power but there is only one side you would ever want to be on, and certainly only one side we would ever want to lead our young athletes into.

Self-compassionate people have been shown to have less fear of failure and are also more likely to try again when they do fail. Since these people are more able to admit their own mistakes and inadequacies, they are more able to embrace accountability for their actions and take ownership of the responsibility for making the necessary changes.

Self-compassion Is Self-indulgent

That self-compassion may be overly self-indulgent is a fundamental misunderstanding of terms.

Self-indulgence is all about having what you want now regardless of the long-term consequences. Self-compassion is about alleviating suffering, not just in the short-term but ongoing. Well-being often requires foregoing pleasure in the present in order to benefit the future self, as in activities such as exercise and healthy eating. So a self-compassionate person would more likely avoid the indulgent behaviours in order to improve their overall, long-term well-being.

A compassionate coach would not allow their athletes to skip training and eat whatever they liked. They would encourage hard work and discipline since that will more likely lead to the players becoming better people and athletes.

Self-compassion Is Narcissistic or Too Self-centred

As opposed to narcissism or self-centredness, self-compassion is not concerned with positive evaluations of one's own abilities or qualities. It generally comes into power at times of pain or suffering. In fact, the self-compassionate person is far more likely to recognise their similarity to others than they are to vainly highlight the ways they are different from or better than others. If anything, this recognition of our common humanity naturally leads us to adopt a humbler attitude to life, which is another building block of a mastery mindset.

Becoming more self-compassionate also has the additional valuable effect of making us more compassionate to others. Bringing positive energy to our own inner world means less stress and anxiety and more energetic space, awareness and empathy for others who are suffering. If we want to bring more warmth and kindness to our interactions with the outer world, we must start by bringing it to the inner one first. This interplay of compassions has important and far-reaching implications for our wider sport culture, which we will delve further into a little later.

Athletes Need Self-esteem, Not Self-compassion

As for the comparison with self-esteem, it is relevant here to address the relative similarities and differences between the two terms. Self-esteem has historically been synonymous with mental well-being, and in fact it is associated with happiness and life satisfaction as well as experiencing less anxiety and depression. But the issues arise not so much with having self-esteem but in getting and maintaining it. Overall, self-esteem is often associated with qualities such as physical appearance or popularity, or outcomes, such as athletic or work performance. Essentially it is rooted in evaluations relative to others. This type of self-esteem can be transient and unstable, only reflecting the latest success or failure, rather than being founded on a deep sense of identity and self-worth.

Self-compassion offers many of the same benefits as self-esteem but without any of the potential downsides. Both offer a sense of self-worth, which is vital for thriving in life and sporting endeavour; but self-compassion offers it from a place of acceptance and security, whereas self-esteem harnesses feelings of superiority and achievement. Kristin Neff and her colleague Roos Vonk conducted the largest study to date, comparing self-compassion with self-esteem in the Netherlands. Surveying over 3,000 people from various walks of life, they found that self-compassion was associated with much more stable feelings of self-worth (assessed 12 different times over 8 months) compared to self-esteem.

In the volatile and unpredictable world of competitive sport it is highly beneficial to base one's sense of self-worth on something more stable than comparisons with others, performance and achievement. Self-compassion offers just that.

Where Compassion Can Take Us

Athletes who are kinder and more forgiving to themselves will not be so badly affected by many of the common, harmful aspects of sport, such as negative body image, fear of failure, fear of negative evaluation and overly harsh self-judgement for making mistakes and losing matches. This attitude would lead to a more positive experience of sport that remains fun and engaging for longer, which in turn would mean fewer athletes dropping out early. Ibtihaj Muhammad is an American fencer with a bronze medal from the 2016 Rio de Janeiro Olympics, where she also became the first American woman to compete in the Olympics wearing a hijab. She spoke about the importance of developing a more positive attitude around her body image – 'As a kid, having bigger legs was always something I struggled with …. But I love my legs as an adult. I embrace my shape and my body. I love the strength in my legs and I know that the stronger I can make them the more efficient I'll be as an athlete.'

This is an important dual-effect. On the one hand, training in self-compassion would help alleviate the unnecessary and often excessive suffering of many athletes going through the inevitable bumps and grinds of an athletic career. Reducing the power of the more extreme negative emotions would, in turn, buy athletes the option of a longer runway in terms of participation. Zoom out and take into view many such individuals and you would start to see a population engaged in activity, in challenge, in teamwork for a considerably greater amount of time.

A compassionate system of development would open up vastly more scope for participation and engagement to those who would otherwise be forced out as *not mentally tough enough*. Some of those saved from a forced, early retirement by this approach might even go on to reach the highest levels in the sport. A tool as powerful as self-compassion for dealing with setbacks could make the difference for many athletes who find themselves considering their options at difficult times in their sporting career. A self-compassionate approach of forgiveness and acceptance can also be a catalyst for better, healthier decision-making. Overtraining injuries and burnout are all too common results of the unforgiving mindset that responds to adversity and suffering by demanding ever harder effort. Treating yourself kindly over the long term is more likely to lead to healthier nutrition, sleep and lifestyle choice.

Along with the improved experience of participation itself, the retirement process would also become on average far more positive, preserving more of each individual's love of sport. It is true that a long career in competitive sport is not for everyone, but it should not come to such a crushing or deflating end with such regularity. A State of Sport Investigation by the Professional Players Federation in the UK surveyed 800 retired elite athletes. The study found that over half of respondents felt that they were not in control of their lives and had concerns for their own mental and emotional health. Crista Cullen was a member of the British hockey team that won the bronze medal at the 2012 London Olympics. She spoke about retiring after those Games at the age of 27:

> *I moved back home to Kenya. When I arrived there was this realisation that you're on your own. I felt lost. It was like I had fallen off a cliff. … It took me six months to find my feet, but I was still looking for that identity.*

Cullen then went on to rejoin the GB team in time for the Rio 2016 Olympics where they won a historic gold medal.

In the vast majority of cases, disengaging from competitive sport should be a straightforward matter of preference and prioritising rather than of pushing the emergency eject button and crashing down to earth. The latter response is more likely to scar the athlete in question and render them far less likely to see their sporting endeavours as a valuable source of self-worth and self-identity.

Becoming more self-compassionate can provide an abundance of emotional resources that the individual can then use to care for, and be compassionate towards, others. A compassionate athlete is a better teammate and a better role model to younger generations and the wider world. Moments of compassion in sport are immensely impactful.

In 2018 the England football team knocked Colombia out of the World Cup on penalties. Gareth Southgate, the England manager, went straight over to console the Colombian player, Mateus Uribe, who missed the decisive penalty kick. A photo of Southgate embracing the distraught player was quickly shared across the internet and evoked a flood of responses admiring his compassion, empathy and integrity. Southgate had himself missed an all-important penalty while playing for England in the semi-final of the 1996 European Championships.

Spanish triathlete Diego Méntrida was a few paces behind his British competitor James Teagle in the final metres of the Santander Triathlon in 2020. Teagle mistook a red banner across a crowd barrier for the finish line and lost valuable seconds crashing into it before regaining his bearings, giving up his lead. Méntrida took the lead, but instead of racing on to claim third place he stopped and waited for Teagle to catch up, allowing him to cross the finish line first, after a handshake between the two men. A video of the incident quickly went viral, and the admiration poured in for the Spaniard. In response to all the positive attention, Méntrida said:

> *This is something that my parents and my Ecosport Triathlon group taught me since I was a kid. In my opinion, this is something that should be considered as a typical situation. I never thought that something like this would reach so far and have so much impact across the media. But I'm proud to receive so much love.*

Sport culture is crying out for a more compassionate approach. We are as inspired by compassionate athletes as we are disappointed by more obviously egotistical, self-centred athletes. Dr David Hamilton, author of *The 5 Side-effects of Kindness*, reports that kindness is incredibly contagious. According to him, a single, simple act of kindness has a ripple effect out to three degrees of separation – all the way out to the friend of the friend of the person who observes the original act.

Hamilton asks, 'So with this in mind, can a small group of dedicated people with compassion and kindness in their hearts change the world?' Now consider the same question when that group of people is comprised of elite athletes around the world, and the group is ever-growing.

Showing compassion for opposition players as well as team-mates sends a powerful message that we are all in this together. The word 'compete' originates from the Latin term *'com petere'* – which means *to strive together*. So according to this defini-tion, competitors are people who strive to achieve something together, com-peting to be the best they can be. In short, we need each other. In recognising that fact we will naturally feel a greater sense of connection and therefore compassion for one another.

In the lead-up to the Sydney 2000 Olympics the Interna-tional Olympic Committee launched a global promotional programme to communicate the core values of the Olympics. The theme of the programme was to 'Celebrate Humanity' and included the following narration to one of the short videos entitled 'Adversary'.

> *You are my adversary, but you are not my enemy.*
> *For your resistance gives me strength,*
> *Your will gives me courage,*
> *Your spirit ennobles me.*
> *And though I aim to defeat you, should I succeed, I will not humiliate you.*
> *Instead, I will honour you.*
> *For without you, I am a lesser man.*

Sport has so much to offer, but it desperately craves a deeper meaning that models the best expression of humanity and highlights our reliance on, and respect for, each other and ourselves.

Chapter Summary

- Athletes often treat themselves far harsher than they would a teammate or friend, and this can have severe detrimental effects on both their performance and their overall experience of doing sport. This approach is fear based, and can be highly motivating; but it would be more effective and far healthier for athletes to cultivate a more self-compassionate approach.
- Self-compassion can be considered as treating yourself with the same kindness, warmth and forgiveness as you would a close friend or family member.
- Self-compassion has three components – self-kindness, common humanity and mindfulness.
- A more compassionate sporting culture would mean participants having a more positive and overall healthier experience of sport, thereby retaining them longer in sport, fulfilling more of what potential there is out there, and improving the experience of transitioning out of sport.
- Acts of compassion in the sporting world are hugely inspirational and send a more positive message that we are all in this together, *com-peting* to be our best.

Key Mental-Emotional Strategies and Practices that Underpin This Virtue

- Developing Self-compassion
- Mindfulness Meditation
- Gratitude
- Love vs Fear Reframing

3 Live with Integrity

I am not bound to win, but I am bound to be true.
*I am not bound to succeed, but I am bound to live up to what light
I can.*

— ABRAHAM LINCOLN

Living with integrity is the surest way to develop self-respect
and the respect of others. From the Latin word '*integer*',
meaning *whole* or *complete*, integrity is about living with
honesty of action and in line with your values, principles and
beliefs. If you live with integrity you can create an inner sense
of wholeness, of being at ease with who you are, knowing that
you are being true to your core self and becoming closer to
your aspirational self. We all know people of high integrity
and can immediately recognise that inherent sense of trust that
comes in any interaction with them. These are the people that
we know will be on time and will follow through with any
commitment they make. Being a person of integrity entails
doing what you say you will do with great consistency. That
is why it builds respect and trust in other people, because they
learn that they will consistently get what they expect. The
profound effect of following this simple rule of keeping your
word and the response it elicits in those around you should not
be underestimated. There comes a powerful sense of inner calm
from having behaviour that matches precisely with your outward

communication. To appreciate the psychological benefits of never having to be out of sync with your commitments, you merely have to call to mind the flustered excuses that tumble out of the person who arrives late to an important meeting. The example of being on time for appointments may seem a superficial one, but it shines a light on something important here. Consistent small acts of integrity, such as being on time to meet friends, are essential to building trust and respect, and their absence cannot be replaced. It only takes a few missed commitments to thoroughly undermine the extent that people feel you can be relied on. Being considered reliable by others, which springs from having integrity, is so valuable in life, as it is a prerequisite to many of the most meaningful experiences.

Muhammad Ali is revered as much for his courage and integrity as he is for his immense boxing skill. At no point was this side of his character shown more starkly than when he refused to be drafted for the American army to fight in Vietnam in 1967. He had everything to lose, including his freedom, but as he understood, even more to gain by living by his principles and morals.

> So when the time came for me to make up my mind about going into the army, I knew people were dying in Vietnam for nothing and I should live by what I thought was right.
>
> I'm giving up my title, my wealth, maybe my future. Many great men have been tested for their religious beliefs. If I pass this test, I'll come out stronger than ever.

The key to living with integrity is in knowing your core values and being able to draw on them in all situations to help guide your behaviour. Values are like compass points that help you find your true path in life, but which you never fully arrive at (no matter how far west you travel, you never can arrive at 'West'). As with many things, increasing your awareness around something helps dramatically with your ability to maintain focus and work with it. We all have a reasonable sense of who we are, what we like and dislike, situations we feel more or less comfortable in and times at which we really thrive. This sense of self guides us along our way, but there can be times where we lack clarity in our self-awareness, where we are led astray by unexpected circumstances, emotional reactions or particularly persuasive people. These are the times when it becomes essential to have a deep knowledge of your personal values, to be able to hold your course and stay true to yourself and the way you *want* to behave.

The Values-Led Path

In sport especially, with all the uncertainty and intense emotions, there are countless opportunities to be tempted away from the values-led path. It is by no means easy to stay on the desired path. It is often marked by intensely uncomfortable feelings, as the pressure mounts and you have to continue to endure nervousness and physical pain. The alternative – taking the undesired, emotion-led path often comes with a quick-fix reward – throwing in the towel before the match is truly over puts an end to the physical exertion and the anxiety. By wrapping the match up quickly, you lose, swiftly turning the unknown into the known, thereby satisfying the ego – but only in one respect and in the very short term. Of course, the medium and longer-term effects on you and your ego are far more negative. You lost the match for one thing, but you must also come to terms with the *way* in which you lost. By giving up you let yourself down and let your emotions and the situation get the better of you. You realise only after the heat has died down that losing the match would have been acceptable if only you had the strength to stick to your plan and compete to the end with dignity. But without the right preparation, the very next time you find yourself in a high-pressure moment, you will not have the skills to be sure to notice it and to hold yourself on the values-led path. It is this kind of preparation, in knowing your values and recognising *in the moment* when they are being challenged, that will enable you to perform consistently at your best.

Referring back to the higher purpose of sport, society needs values-led athletes right now. We must be able to show, beyond doubt, that deep personal and economic investment in sport leads to more positive outcomes for more than a select few. If elite sport is to overcome its own existential crisis then it must show beyond all doubt the positive social effect it has. The power of a positive sporting role model should not be underestimated.

Billie Jean King was one such role model who inspired millions. On her way to becoming the world number 1 tennis player, which she achieved in 1966, she was a powerful proponent of equality for the sexes, not only in tennis but also in society in general. Suffering discrimination from a young age she took on a traditional, male-dominated culture and through the force of her will and her athletic talent was an inspiration to people around the world.

And it is primarily in that power, and the accompanying inspirational stories, that elite sport can truly influence the world in a positive manner. Similarly, sporting figures who model negative characteristics such as poor sportsmanship, cheating and arrogance will also exert an influence on those watching. It is worth asking, who are your role models? Do you look up to them simply for their sporting prowess, or is it also about the moral or ethical character they display, and values they stand for?

As a society, and especially as an industry, we should put the athlete-as-role-model right at the centre of our approach. The same could also be said for how we see and value the role of the coach. Acknowledging the coach's position as a social change-maker would lead us to value the role more and also to give more weight to their own personal development. This approach would require us to create more purpose-led federations, organisations and clubs that will put their responsibility to society ahead of their quest to win.

The issue of diving, or simulation, in football (when a player in possession falls to the ground, faking that an opponent has made contact with them, in order to win a free kick) offers a good case study here. It shines a light on an individual behaviour which is indicative of the downgrading of sporting values in this all-encompassing pursuit of results. There is no question that the diving we have been forced to accept as standard practice is plainly and simply cheating: cheating that is, at best, tolerated by clubs and fans, and, at worst, encouraged by them if it helps the team to win, and is watched by admiring young fans. Any club, coach or federation could easily eradicate this pernicious behaviour from their game if they wanted. Equally, players could decide to live and play by a higher code of ethics and refrain. In the context of a values-led philosophy those that do refrain from diving achieve something far greater than a free kick or penalty; they win greater respect from the people watching, from those playing with them and from themselves as they know they have played fairly. Argentine football superstar Lionel Messi has garnered huge admiration and respect, reaching far beyond the football stadiums. This can partly be attributed to his evident sense of honour on the pitch, which seems to enhance his immense ability with a football.

There are other examples of overt and damaging behaviours and attitudes, to lesser and greater degrees, across the whole spectrum of elite sport. Given the lofty and noble rhetoric around sport's mission and its impact on society, anything short of the highest levels of integrity throughout the system will result in a grave undermining of the potential positive effect.

The Impact of Lacking Integrity

One athlete caught doping can radiate a profound negative effect on those around them.

In 2012, one of the most revered and successful road racing cyclists Lance Armstrong was found guilty of 'the most sophisticated, professionalized and successful doping program the sport has ever seen', according to the US Anti-Doping Agency. He received a lifetime ban and was stripped of all his results dating back to 1998, including his seven Tour de France titles. As Armstrong's intricately built house of cards tumbled down, it had a devastating impact on all those around him, including his friends, family and former teammates, as well as the millions of fans who looked up to and admired him.

A club that is shown to have knowingly broken league rules will lose the respect of their fans, their competitor clubs, and will show the whole league and sport in a bad light.

English rugby club Saracens was one of the most dominant clubs in world rugby during the last decade with three European club titles in four years. In 2019 it was discovered that the club chairman, Nigel Wray, had engaged in private business agreements with key players as a way of getting around the league's wage cap. Saracens was fined over £5 million and docked 70 points, consigning them to relegation from the top English division and losing their main sponsor, Allianz. This was 'the most remarkable scandal the domestic game has ever seen', according to the BBC, which demolished the respect Saracens had earned from its domestic and international competitors and shattered the pride of its own community.

A scandal in an international federation calling into question the ethics and integrity of board members will tear at the very fabric of public trust and appreciation of sport as a whole.

In 2015 a raid by the FBI at a luxury Swiss hotel, where seven people were arrested, brought into the public domain an investigation into widespread corruption within FIFA, the world governing body for football. The subsequent fallout led to 34 current and former FIFA officials and their associates being indicted by US Federal prosecutors for bribery, fraud, racketeering and money laundering. Furthermore, the two most powerful men in world football, FIFA president Sepp Blatter and UEFA president Michel Platini, were found guilty of an abuse of their positions regarding a disloyal payment between the two. They were both banned from all football-related activities for eight years. A survey of football fans' opinions organised in 2016 by Transparency International, an anti-corruption organisation, showed that 98 per cent of fans are concerned about corruption at FIFA and 69 per cent did not have any confidence in the governing body.

These are explicit examples of the lost connection among those involved with that which holds real, lasting value in sport and life. A medal won with the aid of illegal drugs holds a fraction of the rewards to the winner compared to a career of integrity, dignity and respect for and by others.

A club prioritising performance gains over playing by the rules tramples on one of the foundational elements of the game itself: sportsmanship. It fails to see that without the mutual commitment to play by an agreed set of rules sport loses its meaning entirely.

When figures at the very top of sport, those with the most responsibility for upholding sport's good standing in the world, behave dishonestly and dishonourably then such attitudes infiltrate every nook and cranny, and legitimise similar behaviour for everyone further down the chain. With all its power for creating social change, sport in this instance can be among the worst influencers on society.

But there is incredibly fertile ground for building pervasive integrity at all levels of the sports system, perhaps to a greater degree than any other industry. This is due to sport's overt values, deeply rooted in ancient history, and the fact that the practice of sport itself provides unique opportunities for exploring and strengthening the very best of the human spirit.

I have worked for a number of years with a top Danish sport psychology consultant and lecturer at Copenhagen University, Troels Thorsteinsson. In conversations with athletes he uses two graphs to illustrate how the constant high pressure and level of challenge placed on elite athletes can offer unique education and preparation for life after sport.

The first graph represents the range of emotions that most people experience, using any timescale you care to choose – daily, yearly etc.

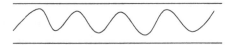

The second graph overlays the emotional range of an elite athlete, with everything that the training, competing and commitment-juggling entails.

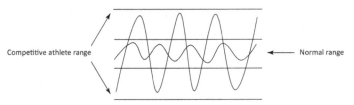

The highs are higher, the lows lower. Those moments of high pressure, filled with emotional threat and uncertainty that must be met with courage and action, become, for the elite athlete, a normal condition. In training to become comfortable with the uncomfortable, noticing when the paths diverge and honing the ability to choose which one to follow, the individual achieves invaluable personal growth.

Everyone playing sport, from the beginner to the Olympian, has the chance to experience the exaltation and discomfort of learning, to grapple with their own limitations, to gain greater understanding of their own inner workings and to feel the joy of developing new skills. The journey of the elite athlete is an unparalleled, relentless series of opportunities for trying, failing and succeeding to various degrees, then reflecting and trying again.

If we see the athlete as the backbone of the global sports body then we can be optimistic about our chances for creating the systems, cultures and values we need. But we must first realise that the overarching priority is in developing athletes of true character with a strong internal moral compass and an awareness of the power and platform they have to make a difference. Making this the priority need not be an uphill struggle. Developing values-led athletes will be essential for the continued flourishing of sport itself and for making sport more socially responsible, but it is also the route to unleashing more of each individual athlete's potential.

A values-led approach highlights for athletes the immense potential, as they go about their day, for developing and strengthening the parts of themselves they hold most dear. This in turn gives an understanding that their true self, the parts of themself they value the most, is not affected by winning or losing. They realise they can be proud of their own performances if they stay true to their values, regardless of the result. This is an incredibly powerful realisation, one that can relieve a great amount of the usual stress around competition and performance as the athlete learns to reduce the significance of the result and put their own effort and attitude at the front and centre of their evaluations.

Integrity as Consistency

Gaining greater clarity of their own values allows the individual to make connections across the various parts of their lives so they can begin to live with more consistency regardless of context. Of course, being an athlete in the heat of competition requires many different traits compared with being a good friend, sibling, student etc., but it can be a concern when a person has wildly different personalities depending on which context they operate in. There is greater strength, and it is evidently more healthy, having a solid foundation of character on top of which to add the necessary traits required for different tasks and environments. If an athlete is mean-spirited, ruthless and unforgiving in their competitive life but laid-back, kind and loving in their social life, they would be well-advised to explore which of those two personality types feels most like their true self (in this case almost certainly the latter, as very few people actually *want* to be mean of spirit). Only then can they work on identifying and incorporating any positive, helpful aspects they can excavate from the personality they want to move away from. Incidentally it was this kind of thought exercise that helped me realise that I didn't really want to make enemies of my competitors. That was far from how I saw myself outside of sport, so why would I uphold that kind of attitude as part of my sporting persona? I decided that the core *me* is someone who would rather build relationships and seek connection with those around me, and of course that includes those I sometimes would have to compete against.

Integrity can also be understood in a structural sense – a building of integrity will stand strong in a storm. An athlete who cultivates an understanding of their own strong foundation of character will be able to withstand conflict without being drawn away from their values and principles. Knowing one's own boundaries, when to stand up against outside pressure without compromising oneself, and being able to say no are all integral aspects of character in a person of integrity. The cyclist who refuses to take illegal performance enhancers or the footballer who refrains from diving to gain free kicks when there is a culture that encourages both behaviours requires both courage and a steadfastness in their own convictions. These strengths can arise naturally in any person, but are far more likely to be found in those who have spent time reflecting on the type of person and athlete they want to be and what they will or won't stand for.

Sport will only truly thrive and reach close to its potential for doing good in the world when it is run by people and organisations with this strong foundation of character, and with a central focus of creating environments and systems that have human development and flourishing at their heart. If this approach can take centre stage, knocking medals and power off the pedestal, then we will notice the athlete experience, from junior all the way up to professional and Olympic level, becoming a far more healthy and motivating one (while of course still highly challenging). We would develop athletes who know themselves better, have their priorities in good order and have a healthy perspective for what really matters in life and sport. Clubs, organisations and national federations would recognise the advantages to be gained in promoting this approach, for the retention of talented young athletes, improved health and well-being of their players and members, and in the improvement of the overall performances. International federations would begin to be filled by a generation of values-led athletes driven by a force far greater than the pursuit of glory and fame – the deep satisfaction that comes from knowing they are living with the utmost of integrity, creating meaning for their own lives and a positive impact on their sporting community and wider society.

Chapter Summary

- Integrity is about maintaining an honesty of action and living in accordance with your values, principles and beliefs. By living with integrity you gain a sense of inner calm and elicit greater respect and trust from others.
- The route to integrity lies in exploring and understanding your own values and boundaries. This work can be of great benefit to an athlete's performance as well as in their life outside of sport.
- The damaging effect of lacking integrity is massive and at the systemic level is the cause of a grave undermining of the public's trust in elite sport.
- Sport offers a uniquely fertile ground for developing individuals and organisations with strong moral compasses. This is precisely what we need to focus on in order to unleash more of sports potential for doing good in the world.

Key Mental-Emotional Strategies and Practices that Underpin This Virtue

- The Athlete Identity
- Knowing Your Core Values
- Mindfulness Meditation
- The Controllables

4 Acknowledge and Embrace Responsibility For Your Own Journey and That of Your Community

With great power comes great responsibility.
— UNCLE BEN, SPIDERMAN

The highest ambition of the True Athlete is not in breaking records and winning trophies, it is in using their strengths and platform to the utmost benefit for society. The greater the performer and the bigger the platform, the greater the responsibility to make a positive impact in the world. This idea sits at the heart of the True Athlete Philosophy: that sport must be about far more than the performances and results, and with its immense potential as a force for good in the world comes the imperative that we must find the way to unleash that potential.

As with the other three True Athlete virtues, responsibility holds significant importance for an athlete in both their sporting journey and their life in general. In sport, taking a high degree of responsibility for your own development is a prerequisite to fully realising your potential as an athlete. In sport and in life, acknowledging and assuming responsibility for yourself, your community and beyond is the surest path to building self-respect and trust in others, and creating greater meaning.

Let us consider an individual's sporting journey. Every athlete is on a pathway from the moment they take up a sport which leads them to take increasing responsibility for their development as they progress. This is the perfectly natural way of things, as a child beginner relies on their parents and coach to dictate when and how they learn the sport. The adolescent athlete starts to take over more decisions about their level of engagement and their own style for playing their sport of choice and their parents will start to step back and give them more ownership. The young elite athlete will be faced with some of their first major life decisions which do not involve their parents and will also be taking the reins for many of the tools and methods for improving their performance. This could be by focussing on physical or mental training, working with a nutritionist to optimise their diet, seeking out feedback or inspiration from different sources. The fully matured elite athlete recognises that they must take responsibility, as far as possible, for everything in their environment. They become like the CEO of their own personal business, ensuring that the people around them (coaches, staff, family members etc.) each know their roles and how they can help most effectively. They create their own vision for where they want their progress to lead, drawing on advice and input from a variety of trusted sources. This advanced level of personal agency requires a strong knowledge of all aspects of performance and brings with it a deep confidence and sense of contentment born of having taken control of the controllables. British Fencing describes this pathway of increasing responsibility to their talented athletes as passing through a series of stages – from student to apprentice, entrepreneur and finally CEO – highlighting the progression of relationships that is an integral part of athlete development. Their Leadership Relationship Model states:

> *Managing relationships is one of the most important differentials for long term success, not just in sport. Yet athletes are often themselves 'over-managed' – by parents, coaches, federations – which will prevent them from developing the skills they will need to be truly successful.*

Some athletes will never fully embrace this responsibility however long they compete, and will limit their personal growth, their sense of agency and their achievements in the process. It is no surprise that the high road is not equally attractive to all, as not all are equally comfortable with the emotional- and ego-related risk inherent in being *responsible*. Under such conditions if things fail or mistakes are made, it is all too clear where the buck stops. The easier route by far is to refrain from claiming such responsibility and to keep hold of the ego's version of a get-out-of-jail-free card when things do not go to plan. However, there are immense benefits available for those that endure the discomfort and embrace their responsibilities.

Within the context of taking responsibility for one's own development some key areas must be closely examined:

- Mistakes and failures
- One's own emotional responses

Taking Responsibility for Mistakes and Failures

In order to learn from your mistakes you must first admit them and accept responsibility for them, or at least accept responsibility for doing the work to ensure they don't happen again. As we have discussed already, there is a threat to the ego when admitting responsibility, in this case for a mistake. We can all recognise the protective armour our egos try to clad us in as we attempt to shift the responsibility to the coach, a teammate, the referee, the weather or anything other than ourselves. If our egos successfully put up that barrier, then hope for any meaningful growth or development is lost. It is necessary to wrangle and negotiate with the ego to keep the armour down, to feel vulnerability and to accept the consequences of the mistake. In return we get a clearer view of the reality of our situation, which we can put to great advantage for our continued development. In the search for high performance, this struggle with the ego in order to take responsibility for mistakes and failures is absolutely pivotal, but is not widely recognised as such. It is, in fact, far more common, even at the highest levels of sport, to see athletes shirking responsibility and attempting to paint a picture of an outcome that was decided by factors entirely out of their control. This is not to say that bad luck and malice never come into play to decide outcomes, but the true frequency of these occurrences is far lower than the competitors concerned would lead us to believe.

As well as embracing the vulnerability that accompanies the ego-threat of admitting mistakes, we have discussed already how a self-compassionate approach can help us to assume personal responsibility in moments of error, failure or inadequacy. In this way the trait of compassion supports the trait of responsibility.

Taking Responsibility for One's Own Emotional Responses

It is important to begin by saying that we are not in control of our emotions. Thoughts and emotions arise in our minds for all sorts of reasons, and are often not those that we would choose for ourselves if we *were* in control. For anyone that has tried the simple, mindful practice of focussing the attention on the breath, and noticing when thoughts and emotions show up, it is as clear as day that we are not in control of our own minds. It is our biology and our conditioning that largely determine our emotional responses to stimuli, not our conscious mind. But we can *gain* control over how we respond to our emotions when they arise. The word 'gain' is significant here because without training, it often feels like our response to an emotion is just as automatic as the emotion itself.

Imagine a player in a game of football. The game is tied and tense, and our player is running with the ball in the midfield, looking for a teammate in a good position to pass to. They spot one of their strikers in acres of space with an open route to goal and are just about to make the pass when they are cynically fouled by an opponent. The referee waves play on. Anger erupts in the player, aimed at both the opponent for playing dirty and the referee who clearly seems against their team. That was their chance to be a key part of putting their team ahead and maybe even the match-winning play. All this goes through their mind in a matter of seconds, and before they know it they are furiously screaming at the referee for not calling the foul (blowing up like this is a well-understood phenomenon, nick-named 'Amygdala Hijacking' by psychologist Daniel Goleman in his book, *Emotional Intelligence: Why It Can Matter More Than IQ*). But the play has moved on and our player has taken themselves out of position and out of the game, giving the opposing team a better chance for the counter-attack. It takes a good few minutes for the anger to subside and for their head to get back in the game, plus they picked up a yellow card for their tirade against the referee! (Research by Jones, Paull and Erskine has shown that players who are perceived as more aggressive will pick up more yellow and red cards on average. Similarly, when a player is perceived favourably the benefit of the doubt will more likely go their way and their transgressions will more likely be forgiven, a point made by Stuart Carrington in his book *Blowing the Whistle: The Psychology of Football Refereeing*.) In this case, while it was the opponent who illegally stopped them making the pass, and the referee who called for the play to continue, neither of them were responsible for the reactions of our player that followed. The anger that arose is a natural reaction to such a raw sense of injustice, but the responsibility for the tirade against the referee and the loss of focus on the task at hand lies squarely with the player. Their inability to deal skilfully with their emotional state caused them to behave in ways that they would never choose, given the chance. Daniel Goleman puts it bluntly: 'Out-of-control emotions make smart people stupid.' This is not a rare case but a situation we can see play out every weekend in every league in the country. This type of interplay between emotions and reactions is repeated for every competitive athlete, at all levels of sport, almost every time they perform, with either constructive or destructive results. It is, therefore, of the utmost importance that any competitor understands which aspects of their performance are within their sphere of control and which are not, grows their awareness of the dynamic between various emotions and their own reactions to them and especially takes responsibility for those reactions in order to enable more consistently constructive outcomes.

More on Complaining

When it comes to complaining – especially in the heat of competition – athletes must recognise an important perspective. Let us take the previous example of the footballer venting their anger over a refereeing decision. First, we must note that complaining after the fact serves no positive purpose, except for the meagre potential gain of putting pressure on the referee to try and influence their subsequent decisions. It will, in fact, be far more likely to push the referee in the other direction, as no one appreciates being aggressively criticised for anything, especially when doing their best at a difficult job. So the complaints will not change what has happened while also putting the referee under pressure. This could actually end up worse for that footballer and their team, and as we saw earlier, it takes valuable attention and energy away from the most important task of playing football.

Now we can add another layer: the mind of the competitor is often clouded by swirling emotions, and especially at moments of perceived injustice. It is a terrible state from which to try to judge a situation accurately. In a significant number of cases, the athlete who complains about a decision will look back at a recording of the incident and recognise *they* were wrong, not the referee. From my own experience conducting hundreds of post-match video analysis sessions with fencers, I estimate that around 80 to 90 per cent of the times where an athlete has complained about a decision, the replay shows that they were in the wrong. In these cases it renders the emotional outburst and the negative after-effects utterly regrettable for the athlete themselves as well as being disrespectful to the referee, their team, fans and opponents. If, in the cold light of reflection, an athlete can recognise that this mistaken victimhood is a distinct possibility should they go down that reactionary path, then it follows that they should make the commitment to refrain from ever complaining during a match or performance. It is rarely a considered choice but rather an emotional flare-up that causes athletes to behave like this. An athlete can psychologically prepare for such emotional situations and be less likely to be drawn away from their values to the point of losing control and thereby losing the respect of themself or others.

The Responsible Life: A Life of Agency and Meaning

The value of assuming responsibility for the important things in life cannot be overstated. This value springs from living a self-determined life, where you take the steering wheel for your own journey rather than handing control over to others, or fate, to decide. It also comes from embracing a certain amount of responsibility for those around you – your friends, your family, your community – and extends all the way up to the natural environments and planet we live on.

Some guidelines to live a more self-determined life:

Proactively commit to take action to change your circumstances or environment. You have more power to influence your experience of life than you may think, so avoid the pitfall of believing that life is something that happens *to* you. Every day you make an enormous number of decisions about what you spend your time doing, and the manner in which you go about doing those things. Within these daily choices lies the power to steer your life in the direction you want. You will be most effective at making changes when you visualise the future and set yourself goals, and then constantly course-correct as you attempt to move towards them. The monitoring and correction of the direction you are travelling require regular self-reflection on how well you are travelling towards your goals and how suitable or valued those goals remain to you. It is natural that your goals may well change as you start to move towards them, which is why it is vital that you reflect on them. It is the movement towards, not the achievement of goals that gives more meaning to life. It would be a shame to achieve a long-sought goal only to realise that you were aiming at the wrong target all along.

Don't blame others for your situation. This creates a sense of victimhood and robs you of the opportunity to make any necessary improvements. There may be times when another person has negatively impacted you, but the act of blaming, in any instance, is focused on judgement and is entirely unproductive. Having someone or something to blame can sometimes feel cathartic, but it holds you captive in the past, and carries heavy and unnecessary emotional baggage. It can be a helpful, logical way of dealing with a mistake or failure, to identify where the fault lay, but it should not be an exercise in passing judgement. Even though something may not have been your fault, it is still your *responsibility* to find your best path forward in any given situation, so that is where you should place your focus.

It is common for people to replace blaming others with blaming themselves for a failure or an unwanted situation. The object of judgement may be different, but the effect is the same, and is equally unhelpful. This act of self-recrimination and judgement seems to be a type of accountability, but it is actually an imposter and has the opposite effect of taking responsibility. The negative emotions associated with self-blame and judgement will hinder any effort to assess a situation honestly and rationally. The resulting blow to self-esteem makes positive change-talk less accessible with the result being self-criticism alone. Once again, crediting the fault accurately and unemotionally, assuming responsibility for making the necessary change and then deciding a positive path forward is absolutely the best way to deal with mistakes or failure.

Analysing problems, standing up against injustice and giving constructive criticism are entirely positive efforts and not to be confused with complaining. The difference between them is that complaining is an end in itself, whereas the other behaviours are all simply steps towards a different end-goal.

As described earlier, it is essential to *refrain from complaining* because it is the catalyst for a downward spiral. Complaining is a replacement for action, and calls attention to a sense of perceived victimhood. Complaining may feel like a useful way of venting or blowing off steam, but in fact it is more likely to make you angrier or more frustrated as you relive the negative emotions. Over time, giving extra weight and attention to negative events leads you to focus more on problems rather than solutions and makes people perceive you more negatively. In sport we are used to hearing complaints from players, coaches and fans. The athlete who regularly complains and vents their negative emotions to everyone around them slowly loses the respect of their team, opponents and others. Australian tennis player Nick Kyrgios is renowned on the ATP Tour for his hot temper. In 2019, after a clash with the umpire at the Cincinnati Masters tournament, he was fined $113,000 for unsportsmanlike conduct, verbal abuse and leaving the court. This was just the latest in a long line of public outbursts for Kyrgios. Rafael Nadal, one of the most revered and respected tennis players of all time, criticised him after a match between the two at the Mexican Open, also in 2019, and a match in which Kyrgios had been booed by spectators after serving underarm. In the post-match analysis Nadal said of Kyrgios: 'He lacks respect for the public, his rival and towards himself.'

Those who deal with resistance and bad luck stoically, without grumbling and without burdening others with their own baggage, grow in the eyes of others and are on the path to becoming dignified leaders in their field. Roger Federer is the prime example; he exudes class and dignity, both in victory and defeat. But amazingly enough there was a time when Federer was every bit as tempestuous and histrionic as Kyrgios. David

Law, who was the ATP Communications Manager at the time when Federer entered the world stage, recalls that early time in Federer's career:

> *The number of times we would go to tournaments and he would throw in a substandard performance where he'd mentally break down or he'd get emotional and throw his racquets – he was a baby.*

Law believes that the death of Federer's childhood coach, Peter Carter, was the primary reason for his dramatic transformation into one of the most admired competitors across any sport. Most people now will only know him for his cool, calm and determined demeanour on court and deeply respectful approach to those around him and the game of tennis itself. In the 2011 Leader RepTrak survey, which assesses the reputations of the 54 most visible public figures around the globe, Federer ranked as the second most respected, admired and trusted individual in the world. He came in just behind Nelson Mandela in the survey of over 50,000 people across 25 countries.

Make a Difference in the World

The year 2020 may have been the final year that the age-old trope of 'stick to playing sports' had any power against athletes who try to make an impact outside of their sporting bubble – thanks, in large part, to a huge swathe of athletes speaking out in response to the Black Lives Matter movement but also to the principles and incredible conviction of then 23-year-old Manchester United and England footballer Marcus Rashford. Rashford almost single-handedly forced the UK government into not one but two high profile and embarrassing policy U-turns involving the provision of free meals to the country's poorest and most vulnerable school children. Having rejected Rashford's plea to keep providing the food vouchers during the summer holidays, the UK Prime Minister, Boris Johnson, and his Conservative Party came under intense public pressure after the footballer wrote an open letter to the government followed by spearheading a hugely popular campaign. Rashford wrote about his own experiences growing up in poverty, relying on free school meals, food banks and soup kitchens to get the food his family needed to live. In his letter he encouraged Members of the UK Parliament to consider the most vulnerable children across the country, 'to hear their pleas and to find your humanity'. The reversal of the government's decision led to the continued provision of food vouchers to 1.3 million children in the UK for the six weeks of summer when the schools were closed. Amazingly Rashford's campaigning brought about a similar U-turn just five months later, forcing the government to promise that food vouchers would be continued in 2021.

In a statement after the initial successful campaign, Rashford said:

> *I stand proud today knowing that we have listened, and we have done what is right. There is still a long way to go but I am thankful to you all that we have given these families just one less thing to worry about tonight. The wellbeing of our children should ALWAYS be a priority.*

We know definitively that the most effective way to create a sense of meaning in life is to transcend your own ego and to be of service to others, the natural world or to the planet itself. In the words of the late Supreme Court Justice Ruth Bader Ginsberg: 'To make life a little better for people less fortunate than you, that's what I think a meaningful life is. One lives not just for oneself but for one's community.'

To create meaning in sport you will also need to connect your journey to something greater, something other than just yourself and your own personal gain.

Owen Eastwood, a performance coach who has worked with some of the world's top Olympic and professional sports teams, wrote the stirring book *Belonging*. In the book Eastwood elaborates on the approach he takes with each team he works with, which involves harnessing the wisdom of our ancient ancestors, and notably his own Māori ancestors, and learning from how they built powerful, cohesive tribes. Being connected to something greater than ourselves represents a central tenet of the Māori culture, described so engagingly by Eastwood through the concept of Whakapapa: 'Each of us are part of an unbreakable chain of people going back and forward in time. Back to our first ancestor at the beginning of time and into the future to the end of time. ... We share a purpose with them. We share a vision for the future. We fit in here ... Whakapapa points a finger at us and tells us, You will not be judged by your money or celebrity or sense of self-pride. ... You will be judged by what you did for the tribe.'

The story of Italian bobsled legend Eugenio Monti epitomises this ability to think beyond one's own personal gain for something far greater. In the 1964 Winter Olympics in Innsbruck, Austria, Monti and his partner were among the favourites in the two-man event. During the competition they were leading their major rivals, the British team of Tony Nash and Robin Dixon, when the British duo broke one of their axle bolts, effectively ruling them out of the event. However, upon hearing this, Monti told the beleaguered Brits that if they could get someone to the bottom of the hill to meet him after his final run, they could have his bolt. After a mad dash by one of the British team engineers, the switch was made successfully, and the British team ended up beating Monti and his partner to win the gold medal. The Italian was a passionate and formidable competitor, but also recognised that victory without honour is not worth all that much. He went on to win both the two- and four-man events at the following Winter Olympics, was awarded the first-ever Pierre de Coubertin medal for fair play and the organisers of the Turin Winter Olympics named the bobsled track after him.

There are many Olympic and World champions who feel a deep sense of anti-climax once they get over the short-lived euphoria of their peak success because they were expecting to finally feel fulfilled. But the result in itself changes nothing about who they are or the relationships that truly matter to them. Medals and trophies lose their shine, sometimes far quicker than we would imagine. They should not, and indeed cannot, be the vessel for our hopes and dreams of fulfilment and self-actualisation.

The True Athlete Philosophy promotes the view that we all have a responsibility to make a positive impact in the world, whether that be in small ways, such as showing kindness to someone in need or volunteering once a week in your community, or in big ways such as Marcus Rashford exemplified. We never know the true impact of the ripple effect of our actions.

US women's soccer captain and double World Cup winner Megan Rapinoe has been a passionate advocate and activist for the causes she holds dear such as women's rights and equality in sport, civil rights and racial justice. In a 2020 interview aired on HBO she said:

> *I believe that we all have a responsibility to make the world a better place. I clearly am very lucky to have a platform to get to play for the United States and be able to take on some of these issues. ... I think that we can live in a more fair and equitable society; I think that we can have a better life.*

As citizens of our countries and of the world we have various responsibilities: to respect our fellow citizens' human rights, follow the laws of the land, pay taxes, vote responsibly etc. With greater advantages and power comes a great responsibility to enact positive change. Sport is a unique training ground for personal growth and provides the context for displays of the most soaring aspects of the human spirit. Those people who stick with sport up through the levels and test themselves against teammates, opponents and nature can give themselves an incredible foundation, both personal and outward-facing, to be great social change-makers.

But even the young competitive athlete can make a positive impact as a friend and leader with their teammates or as a role model to the youngest in their club, if they choose to embrace those aspects of responsibility. The True Athlete Project mentoring programme matches Olympic, Paralympic and elite athlete mentors with aspiring young athlete mentees. They go through a year-long journey of exploration together where the mentee is also encouraged to work on a project to help make a difference to others and their community. One mentee, Souleyman, a 19-year-old visually-impaired sprinter from the UK, inspired young kids by visiting over 100 primary schools to talk about being a visually impaired athlete with big ambitions. Another mentee, British fencer Sophia, introduced the mindfulness she had learned to the younger groups at her fencing club. A third mentee, Leo, a basketball player, took on a campaign to petition his local council in Edinburgh to renovate the dilapidated public basketball courts.

Consider the fact that athletes have great potential to make a positive impact in their community and in the world. Combine that with the fact that this type of service mindset leads to the greatest sense of meaning and fulfilment in life (a mindset typified by the compelling concept of '*servant leadership*', a leadership philosophy advanced by Robert K. Greenleaf in his book of the same name). Recognition of these two facts could provide the necessary impetus to athletes of all ages to look up from the bubble of their personal sporting experience. To connect their journey with something greater, some way of giving back that will make a positive difference, however big or small.

In the words of the tennis legend as well as civil and human rights activist Arthur Ashe, 'Start where you are, use what you have, do what you can.'

If we are to create a better world for future generations, then we each must take some degree of personal responsibility – to play our part. In sport we must recognise the unique conditions and communities that make it possible to lead the way towards this better future. This concept has been envisioned and given lip service by many a leader, but we are still far from unleashing sport's full potential in this respect. We should create a structure of sport and pathways of athlete development that lead participants to this understanding and inspire them to actively engage. We could turn the focus of sport itself much more towards benefitting society as a whole, and co-opt all participants to do their bit to make it a reality.

Remember this. Hold on to this. This is the only perfection there is, the perfection of helping others. This is the only thing we can do that has any lasting meaning. This is why we're here. To make each other feel safe.

— Andre Agassi

Chapter Summary

- Taking responsibility for things that happen to you and in your life is often the source of a great deal of self-respect, trust from others and meaning in life.
- In order to learn from mistakes, one must first acknowledge the responsibility for making them.
- There is a great benefit to an athlete in assuming responsibility for their own emotional reactions, rather than blaming others or unfortunate circumstances. That way they can start to work on choosing desired or wise reactions.
- There is meaning and a sense of fulfilment to be gained from living a self-determined life – proactively committing to take actions in your life, refraining from blaming others and complaining.
- Athletes of all ages and levels have some form of platform, and therefore they are responsible to make a positive impact in the world around them. Connecting their sporting journey to something bigger than themselves is a highly resilient approach.

Key Mental-Emotional Strategies and Practices that Underpin This Virtue

- Knowing Your Core Values
- Gratitude
- Love vs Fear Reframing
- The Power of Nature Connectedness

5   Grow Your Awareness in the Present Moment and of What Truly Matters in Life

Between stimulus and response there is a space. In that space is our power to choose our response. In our response lies our growth and our freedom.

— Viktor Frankl

The Austrian psychiatrist Viktor Frankl survived the horrors of the Nazi concentration camp Auschwitz, and then went on to become the founder of logotherapy. Drawing from what Frankl had witnessed while imprisoned, logotherapy is a form of psychotherapy in which the search for a life of meaning is the central human motivational force. In the quote above, from his awe-inspiring book detailing his experiences in Auschwitz, *Man's Search for Meaning*, he highlights for us the immense power inherent in cultivating a specific type of awareness. The *space* that Frankl is talking about encapsulates both self-awareness and an awareness of the present moment, two sets of skills that if developed can be the keys to a healthier, expansive perspective and a great deal of personal agency and growth.

Awareness underpins all other aspects of the philosophy discussed in this book. You must be aware of your internal dialogue in order to respond *compassionately* in times of suffering. Having an awareness of your values is essential to living a life of *integrity*, and having an awareness of the world around you is a prerequisite for taking *responsibility* for yourself and others. The Buddhist concept of *Vijnana* can be translated into English as 'awareness' but also 'consciousness' or 'knowing'. To be aware is to be conscious or to know. Without awareness we are in the dark, lost.

The whole idea of *awareness* can seem abstract, so it can be helpful to think about there being various types of awareness. Self-awareness and awareness of the present moment are two such types. Then there is an externally focused awareness related to what is happening in the world around you, both in your immediate vicinity and in the wider world. There is also an awareness of what really matters in all that you do, which relates to our individual and collective goals, values and beliefs. This is also closely connected to our awareness of reality, undistorted by our own emotional lens or filter.

These subsets of awareness are just a loose framework, not an exact science, and they are not entirely separate or distinct from each other. Together they provide us with a way to understand how we can think about, and develop awareness, to benefit our lives in and out of sport. We will approach the subject of awareness here as it relates to improving performance, finding greater meaning in the sporting journey and thriving in life generally.

Awareness in Performance

The foundation of working with awareness to improve performance is in becoming more skilful at choosing the desired, logical and wise response to an event. This begins with being able to notice your thoughts and emotions as they arise, how they affect your behaviour and overall mindset and following from that, implementing relevant strategies for use during performance. In training these aspects of your mind you will improve your ability to hold focus and increase the control over your emotions, two of the most valuable functions for the elite competitor. As the founding father of modern mindfulness, Jon Kabat-Zinn said, 'It is not that mindfulness is the "answer" to all life's problems. Rather, it is that all life's problems can be seen more clearly through the lens of a clear mind.'

We must start by disabusing a common, but lamentable, misconception surrounding our response to stimuli. Many people are trapped in the fallacy that it is the events themselves that cause people's reactions to them. The truth is that it is our thoughts and beliefs *about the event* that lead to our emotional reactions, which in turn cause us to behave and act in particular ways – this being a core tenet of the Stoic philosophy. Consider the tennis player who has just given up three match points in a row to let their opponent draw level, an incredibly difficult situation to deal with emotionally. Players will often feel disappointment, frustration and increased anxiety, which will serve to distract them during the next vital points. But neither the fact that the game is now tied and is precariously balanced, nor that they lost three points in a row are what created their disappointment or anxiety. They would certainly have been in tight matches before and have lost big leads before, and surely would know that these are highly possible scenarios in a competitive tennis match. It was instead their own commentary about the situation that created those unwanted emotions to arise. Thoughts like *'That was my big chance to put this away'*, *'How could I have blown such a great lead'* or *'What will people think of me if I lose now'* would have raced through the player's mind and caused a flood of nervousness and emotion to bubble up. Certainly not the optimal state of mind to help them to win the following point and the match. If only they could have caught the situation before those emotions arose and brought themselves back to the focused, determined mindset that helped create that lead in the first place. This is what we mean by the skilful handling of the space between the negative event and the response. What that would look like in practice here is that although those same distracting thoughts would likely still arise, the player would be ready for them, prepared by their training and armed with a strategy for dealing with them in the moment. Some such strategies will be described in Part 3. As an example, the player could have accepted in advance that challenging situations were likely to occur and that they often lead to unwanted or distracting thoughts and emotions. They would have trained the process of letting those thoughts and emotions pass by without being drawn into them or engaging with them. Alternatively, they could have prepared rebuttals to all the thoughts they knew would flare up in difficult moments, thereby taking control of their inner dialogue before the second, emotional wave hit.

At the heart of these types of strategies is developing awareness of your thoughts and emotions during performance and especially at particularly emotional moments, including both the negative and positive. The relief of winning a long rally or scoring a late goal can lead a player or team to relax and let their guard down for the following play.

Such emotionally disturbing situations require an unwavering ability to bring the mind back to the present, to be able to continue to hold focus on the techniques, tactics and game plan that will help you perform at your best. Even in the best-case scenario the mind will most likely momentarily be drawn into the past or future. Therefore, an awareness, in the present moment, of the thoughts and emotions you are experiencing, is perhaps the most valuable skill that an athlete can train. It is often overlooked, however, most likely due to its abstract nature. Most coaches know precisely how to teach a technical skill in their chosen sport but will find it harder to be so concrete in helping an athlete to improve their focus and control their emotions. Indeed, these are often seen as being the remit of the sport psychologist, which becomes a problem as few athletes have sufficient access to such specialist support. Regrettably, sport psychology is still largely underrated and underutilised at all levels of sport. If it were more widely adopted, there would be definite gains in performance, general well-being and mental health. The term *psychologically informed environment*, or 'PIE', describes this kind of thorough implementation of psychological practices and theory within a sporting system – from the leadership through to the coaches, support staff and athletes.

As an athlete you already understand that focused attention is the currency of high performance. The more of that currency an athlete can build up, the better they are able to fulfil their potential. Focused attention and awareness are not one and the same; however, one method of gathering more currency of focused attention is by developing awareness of the inner workings of your own mind and the events and situations that can affect it.

Cultivating a practice of mindfulness meditation is the most effective way of growing this kind of awareness, gaining more currency of attention as well as mastering your emotions. The benefits of mindfulness are not limited to the performance realm, and it therefore has an important role within The True Athlete Philosophy. We will explore the concept in more detail in Part 3.

Awareness of What Has Gone Before, Is Happening Now, and Could Come Next

One of the main reasons that emotional control and understanding the workings of your mind is so important in sport performance is that we are often distracted from what really matters at any given moment, namely the task at hand. As mentioned above, our minds are constantly led astray by biologically determined emotional responses to given situations, and most notably to situations that involve perceived threats or high stress – common in any sports competition. Our brains are not wired to differentiate between threats to our ego and threats to our physical bodies. We end up having the same biological reactions to losing an important match as our ancient ancestors would have done upon seeing a sabre-toothed tiger enter their camp. Our brains are still programmed to operate in a world that hasn't existed for millennia. This demonstrates that in any performance where we care about the result, we are engaged in a constant struggle against our own biological make-up. In many cases, especially in sports where tactics come into play, the real awareness that we are trying to access is an awareness of what has been happening in the game or event – what is our own, personal current status; what is happening around us right now – and to be able to analyse clearly our options in order to select our best tactics going forward. These elements are often being clouded out by our own inner weather system. Emotional control and understanding of your psychology under pressure is part of the solution for this, but there are other avenues to pursue also. Setting goals related to process, behaviour and attitude, use of visualisation, reflection, debriefing and journaling are all powerful tools and practices for gaining more awareness of the performance itself. Some can be done as advance preparation; others after the fact, to identify patterns and hold the performance up against the mirror of one's game plan and goals.

This type of awareness is a foundation for learning, and therefore is of the utmost importance for athletes. Every performance should be viewed as an opportunity to gain information and feedback into the process to decide what to work on and what to improve going forwards. The fact that sport performance is usually highly charged with nerves and emotion means that a huge amount of this information is lost in the heat of the experience. The use of video recording is highly useful for checking back on the reality of what happened, since an athlete's, and even a coach's, memory will often be greatly biased and cannot be entirely trusted for accurate feedback. This is similar to how eyewitness testimony in legal cases is notoriously unreliable. Our reconstructive memory of events is not like a videotape but is rather built up like a patchwork where our brains fill in the blanks in a way that makes most sense to us, not necessarily accurate to what actually happened.

The greater the clarity of thinking during a performance, the better decisions the athlete will make in real time, but it will also provide the groundwork for improved learning from any experience. The athlete that believes they have nothing left to learn will soon find themselves left behind. Constant curiosity and a drive to learn as much as possible from both success and failure are among the surest routes to maximising your potential. On a broader scale, a commitment to lifelong learning is something that provides meaning, improves quality of life and even keeps the brain fitter and healthier into older-age. Compelling support for this comes from The Alzheimer's Association, which promotes lifelong learning for keeping your mind sharp, reducing memory loss and also to delay or possibly even prevent Alzheimer's disease and other forms of dementia.

Awareness of What Really Matters in Sport

In 1990 two British marathon canoeists, Ivan Lawler and Graham Burns, were awarded the highest UNESCO sporting honour – 'The Pierre de Coubertin Award for Act of Fair Play' – for their display at the World Championships in Copenhagen, Denmark. At that race the British pair were favourites alongside the Danish pair of Thor Nielsen and Lars Koch. In the previous World Championships the Danes had won gold and the British silver. At this race, in the final stages with both teams well out ahead of the pack, the British pair were overtaking the Danish boat when they noticed the Danes were having trouble with a dislodged rudder. They could easily have swept past and claimed the gold without the Danes having a chance to catch them. Instead, they stopped up to help fix their opponents' problem. Both boats then picked up the race to the finish line and the Danes ended up beating the British by a single second! Speaking about the incident many years later, Ivan Lawler said that there was barely a thought in his mind to leave their opponents floundering in order to grab the gold medal. He had completely internalised the fact that the true value of the competition was in testing themselves against their fiercest rivals. Winning gold would not have the same meaning if it came without real challenge. Even though he collected five World Championship gold medals throughout his long and outstanding career, Lawler remembers that race as the one he is most proud of.

Winning at sport will not single-handedly fulfil all your needs and desires. Nor will it make you at peace with yourself or bring you long-term self-esteem. This is a common misconception, continuously perpetuated by sport culture and media and that leads to a huge amount of unnecessary suffering. Both those who 'fail' to win gold, as well as those who succeed at coming first, are susceptible to the plight of believing all their dreams will be fulfilled if they can capture that pinnacle result. Finishing second in the Athens Olympics, a result deemed to be 'a failure to win' by many onlookers, was the catalyst for Cath Bishop, the author of The Long Win, who we introduced in Part 1, to explore what the whole experience meant for her and how winners and losers are viewed dramatically differently by society, based on narrow-minded criteria. This journey led her to uncover significant anomalies, contradictions and inefficiencies that stem from putting winners on such a high pedestal, to the detriment of all others. She alighted on the concept of Long Win Thinking as a broader, more effective measure of success over the long-term that could replace our current short-sighted understanding of what it means to win.

The problem is that the vision of glory is so alluring, the promise of achieving what we have trained for and dreamed of for long years shines so brightly. The images we see of euphoric victors in the moments after their victory and the attention and accolades lavished on them afterwards convince us that it must be worth it. But we don't follow their inner experience for the weeks and months before and after. That is where the more important lessons are hidden. The medal, the championship, the victory, does not suddenly transform the athlete into a different, eternally content and happy being. They remain the same person, just with a little extra silverware for their collection and depending on the sport, perhaps some more financial security and more recorded interviews for their portfolio. But these spoils are a poor surrogate for the riches of mind and body that many athletes expect will come their way.

There are countless examples of world-class, gold medal winners who find themselves bereft and sometimes even depressed shortly after their winning event. There comes a sinking realisation, having reached their pinnacle and there being no place higher to go, and are left thinking '*Is that it?*' Johnny Wilkinson, one of the greatest all-time English rugby players, had a sporting career that every young rugby player dreams of. The culmination of this career was in 2003 at the Rugby World Cup final where England was playing against Australia, in Australia. With the score tied at 17-17 and just a matter of seconds remaining in extra-time, Wilkinson scored a drop goal that sealed the victory for England, and all-time legendary status for Wilkinson himself. Speaking of that time, he said in an interview with Shortlist Magazine – 'I walked into the sunset after that game, the credits came up and the next morning I woke up and could not have felt more empty.'

The euphoria of that moment of victory was indeed intense, but it had already started wearing off mere minutes after he made the winning kick.

This is the fate that awaits those who place too much emphasis and expectation on arriving at the destination and have too little appreciation for the journey that took them there and awareness of the truly important things they encounter along the way. Perhaps in striving for excellence they even sacrificed some of those things that would have brought them the meaning and innate self-satisfaction they thought would come from their eventual triumph.

This Philosophy has been created to address some of the elements of an athletic career which can provide that deeper meaning and leave an athlete feeling proud of what they have achieved, whatever their final medal tally or win/loss ratio may be. Such elements are:

- A focus on self-development through identifying and exploring values in life and sport
- Giving back to the sport or community and being a positive role model or mentor for those that come after
- Committing fully and sacrificing personal interest for that of a team, working towards shared goals with aligned values and missions
- Fostering meaningful relationships with teammates, opponents, coaches and other members of staff

It should be patently clear reading through these elements that none of them hinge, even in the slightest, on the sporting results achieved. These elements speak to some of the most intrinsic and deeply rooted fundamentals of what it is to be human – self-improvement and learning, belonging to a tribe or team, being of service to your tribe, and connecting on a deeply personal level with fellow human beings. That is why they hold such a special position in the creation of meaning for us in life and therefore, also sport. The concept of 'winning' is a far more modern aspect of the lived experience. Indeed the original meaning of the word was to labour, toil and gain, and the idea of winning being about victory in a contest only came into popular culture in the mid-1800s. The fact of coming first in a sporting event does not have nearly the same connection to our biological nature and, therefore, holds none of the same depth of meaning to us. This puts the current cultural obsession with winning and winners in a damning light as we have been glorifying and prioritising, to the exclusion of all else, that which will bring us only a fraction of the potential return on our investment and sacrifice.

External Self-awareness

Self-awareness can be separated into *internal* and *external* self-awareness. Having a clear view of yourself is related to a whole host of highly attractive attributes, such as increased confidence and creativity, good communication skills and decision-making, strong relationships, higher personal integrity and being a better leader.

Much of what we have described earlier, including in the section on living with integrity, would fit into internal self-awareness. This type includes how well you know your values, goals, strengths and weaknesses, emotional responses and the thoughts, feelings and behaviours that mediate them. External self-awareness has to do with seeing clearly how others perceive us, and also, therefore, the extent to which we notice the effect of our behaviour on other people.

In a performance setting an athlete would do well to recognise the significant impact that their body language has on their teammates and opponents (and on themself). It can seem too obvious to be worthy of attention, but having awareness of, and control over, the way you comport yourself can improve your chances of succeeding. It can help you gain the respect of your opponents, the officials, those watching and, once again, the respect of yourself.

Recognising the effect you have on others is fundamental to being able to give back in a meaningful and responsible manner, and in being a good role model to younger athletes and any others looking on. You do not choose whether to be a role model or not, but you can choose the type of role model you want to be. Do you want to lead by good example, showing courage and honour in your performances, and humility and kindness off the field of play, or do you want to merely elicit admiration for your sporting gifts and super-confident persona? Both routes could inspire people, but choosing the first option will open the door to deeper connection with others and one's own true self, while option two will bolt that door closed and limit the potential good that the athlete in question can have.

All athletes have a platform to influence others around them and, as described in the earlier section, that comes with a degree of responsibility to use that position to positive effect. Athletes who have trained mind and body to a higher degree than average can make a comparatively greater contribution in the world. They will also satisfy a deep, human longing for something that connects them with others and gives them purpose beyond their own self-interest.

Awareness of How and Where to Find Support

In my own tumultuous 2012 Olympic year, described in the prologue, two people in particular helped me get through it. Katie, the sport psychologist whom I also mentioned earlier, was one. The other was our team physical trainer, Rhys Ingram. For four months while I was unable to do any technical fencing training while my broken wrist was healing, every day I came into the training centre in Lee Valley, North London, to do strength and conditioning sessions with Rhys. His unwavering commitment, high spirits and focus on giving me the best possible training were a much-needed source of motivation for me at a time where motivation was in scarce supply. Without Rhys and Katie as well as our team physio (a high-energy, affable guy called Ed Mias), my mum and a number of others, I am sure I would not have been able to keep it together and recover in time to qualify for the Olympics.

The journey of an athlete aiming for the elite level is guaranteed to be a rollercoaster. There is no way of avoiding the pitfalls, struggle and challenge, indeed that is part of what makes it meaningful. The ability to seek and find support in times of need can be considered an essential skill of an elite athlete. Nobody reaches the top without help along the way, be it from a coach, a sport psychologist or a kind and caring friend. Support comes in many forms, and it is worth taking time to consider who you have around you that can be there for you in times of need. The traditional culture of sport has emphasised physical, technical and tactical development, and the routes for seeking support in those areas are often more clearly defined for that reason. The emotional and psychological experience is every bit as important to an athlete, but the pathway for finding advice or support for this is far less obvious. There is much work to be done by sporting institutions and organisations to redress this imbalance. For a start, we must strive to fully disabuse the notion that working on your mental skills or mental health is a sign of weakness. It takes strength and courage to admit that something is not optimum and to seek help in addressing it. Talking through issues with someone who cares can go a long way, and as a culture we want every person who is struggling with a mental health concern to reach out and start the process of healing and flourishing once again.

Deja Young is an American Paralympic track and field superstar who won gold in both the 100 m and 200 m T46 classification at the Rio 2016 Paralympics. But the intense pressures of being an elite athlete, coupled with studying at a university led her on a downward spiral. She says:

> *I felt like I was in this hole I couldn't get out of. It just felt like I was getting deeper and deeper. It wasn't until my second semester of my sophomore year that I realized that things were*

getting worse and I didn't really know where to turn … I felt
like no one was going to see my depression or understand what
I was going through. At that point in time, I found that it was
really hard for me to reach out. I was really embarrassed and
felt like any resource I used somebody else needed it more than
me, which is completely false.

Young's condition deteriorated until she was admitted into a psychiatric institution just four months before the Paralympics. As bleak as it was, seeking help there started her on the road to recovery, including a newfound appreciation for asking for help. In her words, 'I still have my tough days, but I am no longer embarrassed or ashamed to reach out.'

This is not just about supporting the psychological but also the *emotional* realm. In the world of high-performance sport where everything is fast-paced with constant pressure to improve and perform, there is a growing recognition of the need for spaces where athletes and coaches can explore their own successes, failures, anxieties and doubts. A place where they can share their vulnerabilities and hear them reflected by others, where they are not there to perform but rather just be themselves. This kind of work on the emotional realm of an athlete's experience forms an integral part of what world-class athlete welfare looks like. At the time of writing (2020–2021), the world is in the midst of the Covid-19 pandemic. For athletes this means cancelled and postponed competitions – most notably the Tokyo Olympics – shuttered sports clubs and fitness centres, and a near-permanent state of training at home, alone. The emotional toll that anxiety, uncertainty and the constant struggle to find motivation takes on athletes has become increasingly evident. Even if the Olympics goes ahead as planned in 2021, it will still be an incredibly stressful period for those athletes who have their sights set on participating.

Fears about contracting or spreading the virus, athletes falling ill at the last minute and having to withdraw, awareness of the ongoing suffering in their communities and around the world all goes to highlight the importance of being able to get athletes the support they need in this respect.

An understanding of the emotional exposure and risk to the ego inherent to high-performance sport is also highly beneficial to performance. Athletes experience many highly uncomfortable moments during performances where they have something on the line, and they must find a way to meet the sheer uncertainty of the situation with courage. The alternative is to respond to the discomfort by seeking an exit as fast as possible. The route to gaining this awareness is the same as mentioned earlier: explore one's own emotional responses and prepare for those moments when the responses are likely to be triggered. A deeper dive into this topic comes in Part 3, under the subject of 'embracing vulnerability'.

The Scholar Athlete and the Wider Context

Think lightly of yourself and deeply of the world.
— MIYAMOTO MUSASHI, JAPANESE MASTER SWORDSMAN AND
PHILOSOPHER

Athletes are prone to becoming wrapped up in the bubble of their own sporting existence, thinking that their worth as a person is based on their results as an athlete, which can lead them to catastrophise issues relating to their performance and sense of self. In this state, underperforming in a tournament can cause days or weeks of despondency, as the failure takes on a disproportional meaning for the athlete relating to their motivation, how they think others will see them and even their overall future prospects in the sport. Having a wider perspective is generally a very healthy approach and one which can also be incredibly beneficial to performance. A far cry from the worn-out adage that athletes should just 'stick to their sport', there is much to be gained from having passions and interests that can allow the individual to burst out from their bubble and see their experience with more clarity and from an elevated perspective. A wider perspective allows the athlete to take a more rational approach and understand the true nature of their experiences. In the case of the athlete who underperforms and starts on the downward spiral, they can recognise that underperformance happens even to the greats. They can then begin to put their experience in a more reasonable context, save a whole lot of suffering and get on with the task of improving their performances. Similarly, if they can put their own plight in comparison with real-life struggle and suffering, they may recognise that what they are experiencing does not warrant such depth of destructive emotion.

It does not even have to be a dramatic comparison to elicit the desired effect. The simple act of asking their coach about how things are with their family and hearing the stories of lives being lived oblivious to the goings-on at any sports event can help to elevate the perspective of a competing athlete who is suffering with nervousness. In the light of normal human existence with all its daily bumps, grinds and struggles, the result of a sporting contest pales in significance and can be seen, even if just momentarily by the competitors themselves, for just what it is: a game. This is not to say this should be a permanent attitude, but that simply being able to access it at times of excessive suffering can be a great help. An ability to see things with perspective is a key building block of overall resilience.

The example set by NFL quarterback Colin Kaepernick, in 2016, still reverberates around the world many years later. This was a vivid example of an athlete seeing their experience through a lens with wider perspective. Kaepernick took a knee during the national anthem that was played before NFL games in order to protest racial inequality and police brutality in America. He opted for the act of kneeling after a conversation with a former NFL player and Green Beret, Nate Boyer. Boyer told Kaepernick that soldiers kneel at the grave of their fallen comrades. Kneeling was therefore intended as a respectful form of peaceful protest for Kaepernick. The protests spread throughout the league, including the whole Dallas Cowboys team plus their owner, Jerry Jones, taking the knee before a game in 2017, then the whole country and into other sports around the world.

Another important trait to cultivate is gratitude for what you have in life. According to a leading sport researcher Dr Nicole Gabana, an increase in gratitude is correlated to higher well-being and a decreased chance for psychological ill-health. Being grateful positively impacts the life of any person, and for athletes it has the added benefit of leading to the widened perspective that we have just discussed. An athlete struggling under the intense pressure of competition could adjust their viewing angle and adopt an attitude of gratitude for the opportunity to represent their community, club or country and the chance to test themselves, competing with a healthy body and mind against a worthy opponent. *Pressure is a privilege* is an elegant way to summarise this switch of attitude and will allow athletes to access a more performance-ready mindset.

In the perspective of this Philosophy, a scholar athlete is one who learns about the context in which they operate and the history of their community. First, this is an expression of the passion for the sport itself – they are so interested that they want to know more about those that came before them, and to find out about the history of the sport itself. A student of Judo would do well to know that Judo was founded by Jigoro

Kano in the 1880s as a method to refine body and soul and to perfect oneself in order to contribute something of value to the world. This is the founding principle and tradition into which the Judo students enter, and being ignorant of it would be a loss for both student and sport.

Knowing the current goings-on in the sport is a sign of curiosity and willingness to learn. This could exhibit itself in studying videos of the best players and learning techniques from them. It could be taking an interest in the ways the sport is run, how diverse and inclusive it is, or the environmental impact and policies that it has. Those who give the most energy to an organisation or movement are also those who should have the most say in how it is organised and the direction it is heading. We are currently seeing a growing number of organisations representing the athlete voice – Global Athlete and Athleten Deutschland to name two such recently founded organisations – who are taking on the traditional powers-that-be in sport.

Having an appreciation of what is happening in the world around you – especially where you are most engaged – provides soil in which you can cultivate activism and social change. Without awareness of the current state of play and the most pressing issues, there is no fertile ground for these plants to grow. NBA star LeBron James is one of the most inspiring exemplars of the ethos of using his platform to advocate for causes he is passionate about. But even he has come under plenty of criticism for being outspoken, including from the unlikely source of a fellow global sporting icon, footballer Zlatan Ibrahimovic. In an interview where he was talking about James, who he expressed a lot of respect for, Ibrahimovic also said: 'I don't like when people with a status speak about politics. ... Do what you're good at doing ... do what you're best at, because it doesn't look good.' Responding to the comments, James hit back: 'I will never shut up about things that are wrong. I preach about my people and I preach about equality, social justice, racism, voter suppression – things that go on in our community … I'm their voice and I use my platform to continue to shed light on everything that might be going on, not only in my community but in this country and around the world … I speak from a very educated mind. I'm kind of the wrong guy to go at, because I do my homework. … There's no way I would ever just stick to sports, because I understand this platform and how powerful my voice is.'

James is the epitome of the scholar athlete, who knows his history, knows the context he is operating in and has a keen awareness of the power of the position he holds. He is determined to use the platform he has gained through his prowess with a basketball to make a far bigger impact, beyond just on the scorecard.

In the words of firebrand sports journalist and social commentator Dave Zirin, writing in *The Nation*, 'We need outspoken athletes, connected to social movements, to speak directly to the masses of people who have tuned out politics.'

And like LeBron James, in order to make a positive mark in the world you will first want to educate yourself about what action is required and where, before deciding how you can best put your efforts to good effect.

Chapter Summary

- Cultivating an awareness of the thoughts and emotions that arise during performance is one of the most valuable pursuits an athlete can devote themselves to. It is the first step to being able to choose wiser responses to events.
- An awareness of what is happening during performance, unclouded by an emotional overlay, is the foundation of making good decisions in the moment, and of learning.
- Achieving results in sport will not alone create a sense of fulfilment. For that one must pay more attention to the developmental journey and especially to the human connections made along the way.
- No top athlete is completely self-made. Being able and ready to seek help and support from others along the way is essential, both for reaching top level performance and for encouraging a healthy approach.
- For an athlete to connect their journey to something bigger and outside of themselves and to become an advocate for causes they believe in, they must first educate themselves as to what is happening in their community or the history of it.

Key Mental-Emotional Strategies and Practices that Underpin This Virtue

- Mindfulness Meditation
- The Controllables
- Embracing Vulnerability
- Reflection

MENTAL-EMOTIONAL STRATEGIES AND PRACTICES FOR CULTIVATING THE TRUE ATHLETE VIRTUES

6   Introduction and Mindfulness Meditation

Introduction

Drop by drop is the water pot filled. Likewise, the wise man, little by little, fills himself with good.

— BUDDHA

In Part 3 we discuss the mental tools and practical exercises that will help you develop and train the virtues of a True Athlete. This is really where the practical aspect of this Philosophy comes into force as we describe precisely how you can work with each element and how they fit into the landscape that we have depicted so far. This section is inspired by the Stoic philosophy, which has its own set of mental-emotional strategies for followers to incorporate into their daily lives. In selecting the right elements for the purposes of the True Athlete Philosophy, we have looked to Stoicism and Buddhism, which were introduced in chapter 1, as well as sport and positive psychology. Positive psychology, first coined by American psychologist Martin Seligman, concerns itself with 'the good life'. Studying positive experiences, traits and institutions, it is focused on individual and societal well-being.

For a philosophy to become practical it must be practised. In the words of author and philosopher Jules Evans:

Greek philosophers had this idea that philosophy has to be a daily practice. It can't just be this kind of French existentialist idea of a nice conversation once a week in a café. It has to be a kind of daily practice. With practice, your philosophy becomes automatic habit, it becomes ingrained.

Each of the elements that follow will require practice, or consistent practical application, if they are to make a difference in your life. Focus is critical when taking on new habits or perspectives. Therefore, it is recommended that after reading through this section, you decide which one or two tools, practices or strategies you will focus on, and then set a time period for implementation. After that you may choose to continue with the same techniques or move on to other practices. Habit-building experts, such as Charles Duhigg, author of *The Power of Habit*, suggest that, as a rule of thumb, 30 days is a minimum period to spend adjusting to a new habit or perspective, though the optimal amount of time will differ, depending on the person and context. Some of these strategies, for example some self-compassion exercises, will need to be trained during moments of pressure during a performance, so will require a number of trials and likely far longer than 30 days to become accustomed to. Others, for example the gratitude practices, can be repeated daily and a significant effect can be noticed within 30 days.

The key thing to remember here is that champions are made by placing one brick at a time, across a broad range of areas. Even the greatest NFL quarterback of all time, Tom Brady, went through a similar bit-by-bit developmental process on the way to becoming a legend of the game:

When I showed up as a freshman in high school, I didn't know how to put pads in my pants…And then when I got a chance in college, I just wanted to play at Michigan. When I got drafted by the Patriots, I just wanted to play, I just wanted to start. It's just been a series of steps like that of trying to be a little better every year, trying to learn a little more every year, trying to grow and evolve in different areas.

Mindfulness Meditation

Meditation is not about having yet another new strategy of self-help plan, but rather providing a framework in which to see yourself more clearly. To begin with, we get distracted a lot. Over time, we get distracted less. Be gentle with your approach, be patient with the mind, and be kind to yourself along the way.

— ANDY PUDDICOMBE

Mindfulness, while still far from mainstream, is becoming ever more prevalent in performance sport, as well as other spheres such as the military and the performing arts. This growth formed part of the movement which led *Time Magazine* to put 'The Mindful Revolution' on their February 2014 cover. What was once considered primarily a spiritual or religious practice is being recognised as a unique and highly practical mental training technique that has significant benefits far beyond just the performance. A meditation programme run by the Holistic Life Foundation is being used to help at-risk high-school students in Baltimore develop tools and skills to help them through life. The US military is also a frontrunner in its use of mindfulness and meditation techniques for optimising well-being and performance. In collaboration with the Army Medical Research Department, Dr Amishi Jha has created a programme called Mindfulness-Based Attention Training, to train military staff to be able to deliver mindfulness classes throughout the military.

Practised for thousands of years across multiple cultures, mindfulness meditation has its roots within many of the world's biggest religions, but the modern, Western conception of it was largely inspired by the Buddhist tradition. Mindfulness is one of several types of meditation, with examples of others being 'mantra', 'movement' or 'transcendental'.

Mindfulness is about directing the attention towards the physical sensations, thoughts and emotions that arise within yourself, moment by moment and without judgement. It is being fully present and aware of what is happening for you, what you are experiencing in the here and now without becoming overly attached or caught up in it. By cultivating this ability of interested detachment from the constant flow of thoughts and emotions that arise, you can start to experience more of the fullness of each moment, without being swept away.

Some of the key qualities that underpin a mindfulness practice are openness, acceptance and curiosity: openness for the full spectrum of experiences that a human can have; acceptance for whatever is arising for you in the moment, without needing to change it and without judging yourself for it; and curiosity – becoming interested in how your mind works and observing your inner experience in all manner of situations, almost as if you were an engaged outsider looking in.

Mindfulness, however, is not just the experience you have when you sit quietly for 10 or 20 minutes to meditate. It is a way of life, where you try to bring a greater sense of awareness and presence to your everyday experience. Whenever you bring an awareness to what you are currently experiencing, you are being mindful. When you are more present and notice more clearly what is happening inside your own mind, you are better able to respond calmly and wisely to emotionally charged situations. This is not to say that mindfulness can eliminate difficult and uncomfortable thoughts and emotions. It *can* help you to recognise them and address them with gentleness and acceptance, as opposed to either giving them free rein to direct your behaviour or trying vainly to suppress them.

The ability to be present, and therefore in control of our responses in times of high emotion, rather than simply reacting, can be a superpower. Speaking personally, this is the aspect of my training for the Olympics that I feel I benefit from most in my day-to-day life since retiring from my sport. Across my work, family and social lives, this kind of inner awareness and an enhanced ability to choose my responses more wisely is put to use every single day.

By now you will hopefully have noticed the central role that mindfulness plays in the True Athlete Philosophy. Mindfulness is both a practice and a trait, and as a trait it forms the foundation for cultivating each of the True Athlete virtues. The central purpose of mindfulness is to increase *awareness* of our inner and outer lived experience. As we have seen, it is one of the three pillars of self-compassion, which helps us to recognise our shared humanity and gives us cause for greater outwardly focused *compassion*. It underpins our ability to choose wisely and stay aligned with our core values at times of stress and emotion, allowing us to go through life with *integrity*. An enhanced recognition of the common experience for all people, of wanting to increase happiness and avoid suffering, leads us to embrace our *responsibility* to do our part in creating a greater good. Furthermore, many of the strategies and tools in this section involve a degree of mindfulness – gratitude, acceptance and defusion, embracing vulnerability to name those with the clearest connection.

When it comes to the monumental task of creating a more compassionate culture of sport, we must bring our focus back to the day-to-day actions we can take to help us achieve our aims. Bringing a greater level of collective mindfulness through a simple and regular practice would send immeasurable positive ripples out into the world.

> *If every 8 year-old in the world is taught meditation, we would eliminate violence from the world in one generation.*
> — THE DALAI LAMA

Misconceptions around Mindfulness

Before we move on to the benefits and practices of mindfulness let's look at some of the most common misconceptions. These misconceptions often present themselves in individuals as resistance or disinterest in exploring mindfulness, so it is important to clear these up in advance to reduce the friction as much as possible.

Mindfulness is a spiritual or religious practice. While it originated from religion and many still practice it in that respect, there are modern interpretations of it which are non-spiritual and non-religious. It is these practices we are presenting here and which are most widely adopted within performance environments.

The goal of mindfulness is relaxation. The overall purpose of mindfulness practice is to increase awareness of what is happening in your experience right now, and to improve your ability to direct and hold your attention, allowing you to choose what you focus on. Relaxation is a common effect of practising mindfulness, but it is not the goal.

It is about emptying your mind. An empty mind is not the goal of mindfulness, but the practice can lead to the pleasant experience of having a quieter or calmer mind. Rather than trying to empty the mind, the idea of mindfulness is to notice more acutely what is happening in the mind, when thoughts and emotions arise and disappear again, and to refocus your attention where you choose.

It takes a long time. The evidence shows that to get the benefit of mindfulness you only need to practice for as little as 10 to 15 minutes each day. There are different levels of experience, and different feelings that come through practising for longer stretches, which can be great fun to explore, but not essential.

It takes a long time to notice any of the benefits. There are benefits that come from a sustained and consistent practice; but there is also plenty of opportunity to notice both big and small differences right from the very first session. For instance, when trying mindfulness for the first time, I had this huge sense of revelation when I realised just how much of my mind's activity comes seemingly at random and in direct contradiction to what *I actually wanted* to focus on. Suddenly I realised that all those random thoughts do not represent me, but rather some complex subconscious processes that I neither understand nor choose.

There is a Buddhist phrase that sums this up nicely: 'the monkey mind'. It refers to the restless, fanciful, inconsistent, uncontrollable part of your mind. It can be useful to think of a monkey character in your mind controlling a lot of your thinking, and making you react in ways that you don't choose or appreciate. You can learn skills and techniques for quieting or controlling your monkey mind, but it is always there, part of you.

Dr Steve Peters, a British consultant psychiatrist who has worked with a wide range of world-class and professional athletes, developed The Chimp Model to help performers understand the inner workings of their mind. In his model there is You – the human, rational part of your brain; The Chimp – which 'thinks' independently and highly emotionally; and The Computer – which is based on deeply coded learning and beliefs and acts automatically or instinctually. Each actor in this model has different speeds of reaction, with the computer being the fastest, the chimp next fastest and the human lagging far behind. This model can be very helpful in explaining why your behaviour can be hijacked at times of high stress or pressure, as the chimp or computer take over before the human can act.

It is this monkey mind that causes most of the trouble for athletes around performance anxiety, distracting and unhelpful thoughts, negative self-talk etc. Mindfulness is one of the most effective techniques at helping you manage your monkey mind, and that is why it is perhaps the single most valuable mental skill to hone, both for life and for performance.

Benefits for Athletes

> *The benefits of mindfulness practice as applied to sports are almost blindingly obvious. Focus, awareness, clarity of thought and the ability to stay in the present moment are basic skills for any great athlete – and meditator.*
>
> — SOREN GORDHAMER

Every athlete is familiar with the concept of being 'in the zone', also famously described by Hungarian-American psychologist Mihaly Csikszentmihaly as being in 'flow', which is the optimal state for an athlete during a performance. This state often involves losing track of time as you are totally absorbed in the task at hand, seemingly effortlessly in total control, fully alert and operating almost subconsciously. This feeling is an intensely enjoyable one, as the levels of challenge and ability are perfectly matched, pushing you to reach the upper limits of your powers. There is little doubt that this is the state athletes want to be in when they compete, but it is near impossible to guarantee accessing that state with consistency. For one thing, the level of challenge must be just right, not too hard nor too easy in relation to your own ability. Many of the other aspects of flow, such as operating subconsciously or time slowing down, are also not within our sphere of control. The single most important thing that we can assert some control over, aside from choosing the correct level of challenge with clear goals attached, is to train ourselves to be more present with focused attention. A key indicator of being in flow is total and utter absorption in the now, which is also the reason that time can speed by without you noticing it. Therefore, the more present you are able to be, without being drawn into thoughts about the past or future, and without ruminating or judging your own thoughts and feelings, the more likely you are to 'drop' into an experience of flow.

I have been lucky enough to experience flow many times during my competitive fencing career, including on some of the biggest stages – Europeans, World Championships and Olympic Games. The time that stands out most for me when I think back was the Senior European Championships in Kiev, Ukraine, in 2007, where I won my first top-flight medal, winning silver. It came almost completely out of the blue considering my previous results at that level. I found my stride towards the end of my first match against a strong Russian opponent, and then the stars seemed miraculously to align. My performance took flight and I proceeded to knock out two legends of the sport, both Italians, who were still in their peak years, one after the other. Everything seemed to come so naturally, and I felt two steps ahead at any moment in the action. Neither of those fights was even close. It is still a bit of a mystery why I hit flow that day. I didn't do anything special to prepare myself for it. It would have had something to do with the decreased pressure that came from being matched against someone so highly rated, coupled with a belief in my own potential and an excitement to show what I was capable of. The nature of the flow state is that it is always somewhat mysterious. I can still put myself back there, feeling the pure joy of performing at my best, and it became the benchmark that I would strive to reach for throughout the rest of my career. That day will forever represent for me the immense potential there is in achieving a flow state – a totally unrivalled feeling.

Mindful Sport Performance Enhancement is a mindfulness training programme developed for athletes by a team of psychologists and mindfulness teachers, based in the United States and led by Dr Keith Kauffman. Kauffman and his colleagues propose that mindfulness can develop a number of key performance facilitators – factors which can contribute to improved performance. These performance facilitators combine to enhance the ability to regulate both your attention and emotion. Being skilful in regulating attention and emotion will better enable you to access experiences of flow and, therefore, achieve peak performance.

Those key performance facilitators are:

- **Concentration** – being able to skilfully shift your attention to different points and hold it there without distraction for longer.

We have already discussed how attention is the currency of high performance, and mindfulness is the best training technique for becoming rich in this currency. The process of practising mindfulness, of consistently refocusing your attention after being distracted, is akin to doing reps in a gym to strengthen a muscle. Your concentration is like a muscle, so it makes sense that finding a way to strengthen it will be hugely valuable to you in your performances.

- **Letting go** – learning to recognise the inherent flux and impermanence of all things and, therefore, being better able to accept things simply as they are now.

When you care deeply about your performance it can lead to an intensity of emotion, which can be a good thing, but can just as easily become distracting. When under pressure, unhelpful thoughts and feelings run through your mind unbidden and seemingly constantly. The ability to let these go by without leading you astray and retrain your focus where you want it to be – on your game plan, on the job at hand – are essential parts of being able to perform when it counts most.

- **Relaxation** – being able to reduce tension and arousal in both mind and body, helping us to think more clearly and our muscles to recover more quickly.

Even though the purpose of mindfulness is not relaxation, the practice can be relaxing. It is important to have tools or strategies to be able to adjust the level of arousal or nervousness you feel. There are many mindful exercises that can be used leading up to and during performance that bring you into a more relaxed state. Furthermore, certain mindfulness exercises, such as the body scan (described later in this section), have been shown to aid recovery after training.

- **Harmony and rhythm** – finding inner balance, a synchronicity with teammates, and a fluid, flexible approach to ever-changing surroundings.

The mindful practice of letting thoughts and emotions pass through your mind like clouds drifting past a mountaintop allows you to continue your performance with far greater rhythm. You are less distracted and less reactive, which brings you to a state of equilibrium and balance. This equilibrium can hold you steady, allowing you to surf the waves of adversity and challenge, rather than be tossed around by them. Approaching interactions with others mindfully with an awareness of your own inner state leads to a deeper connection and understanding.

- **Forming key associations** – creating a series of prompts within training or performance which reminds us of the need for being mindfully aware – for example, a runner setting an alarm to sound on their watch at regular intervals.

This concept will be discussed in more detail later in this section, where they are called *process mantras*.

The evidence shows that mindfulness has potential benefits for athletes on a range of valuable skills and qualities, all of which are heavily linked to the holy grail among sport performers – being in the zone – the exhilarating, effortless and timeless state of total absorption in the task.

For this reason alone, dedicated athletes should practice mindfulness, but when you add in the plethora of health and well-being benefits that are on offer aside from the performance advantages, it becomes almost irresponsible to ignore!

In 2012 Pete Carroll, head coach of NFL team, the Seattle Seahawks, brought in sport psychologist and mindfulness coach Michael Gervais to work with the players. In an interview with ESPN, left tackle, Russell Okung said:

Meditation is as important as lifting weights and being out here on the field for practice. ... It's about quieting your mind and getting into certain states where everything outside of you doesn't matter in that moment.

With this more mindful approach, the Seahawks went on to win their first-ever Superbowl in 2014.

Benefits for All

The mental and physical health benefits of mindfulness sound almost too good to be true, but there is a strong and constantly growing scientific evidence to support them. A comprehensive review of the research into mindfulness featured by the American Psychological Association stated that 'Overall ... the psychological and physical health benefits of mindfulness meditation are strongly supported by research'.

Mindfulness has been shown to reduce negative emotions, rumination and overall stress levels and to boost the immune system and even to grow the amount of grey matter density in areas of the brain linked to learning, working memory, cognitive flexibility and emotional regulation. We have already seen that mindfulness is a key component of self-compassion and developing compassion for others, but it can also help to improve sleep, reduce chronic pain and is increasingly used to treat mental-health conditions such as depression, anxiety and even post-traumatic stress disorder. The Operation Warrior Wellness programme, run by the David Lynch Foundation, has enrolled over 10,000 American military veterans suffering from post-traumatic stress disorder and their families to help promote well-being and resilience.

Improved emotional regulation means that meditators are less emotionally reactive, which combined with increased self-awareness, has been shown to have positive effects on their relationships with others. Mindfulness can help to protect against the emotionally stressful effects of relationship conflicts, leading to a higher level of relationship satisfaction.

On a more mundane level, engaging in a mindfulness practice means you need never be bored again, or not for long at least. As soon as you notice the thought of being bored, rather than resisting it or lamenting it, you can instead turn your full attention to the experience, bringing a sense of curiosity to it. You can only be bored for as long as you are thinking the thought 'I am bored', so when you have some other focus for your attention, such as noticing the precise flow of thoughts going through your mind, or the physical sensations in your body, then the boredom naturally dissipates.

Becoming more aware of our present moment experience can help us to appreciate the world around us more and understand ourselves better. We can learn to bring a 'beginners mind' to our experiences. This is another concept from Buddhism that describes bringing an open, curious and fresh mindset to something that we otherwise might experience on autopilot.

Getting less caught up in the stream of thoughts and emotions, thereby reducing their control over you, and being able to choose your reactions to events more consciously and wisely can be the key to reducing stress and anxiety and enhancing your overall well-being.

Mindfulness is not the answer to all our problems, but it does have a tremendous potential to be a driver for real positive change, from the individual right up to the societal level.

The Second Arrow

The Buddhist parable of the second arrow is a helpful one for understanding the way we can often react to unwanted situations and cause ourselves more suffering in the process. In this parable, the first arrow is the event itself. This can be anything that causes you emotional distress or pain, for example being delayed in traffic or making a game-changing mistake in sport. The second arrow is our own response to the first arrow. It is the story we tell ourselves about the event, the reflexive worrying, anxiousness or self-blame. The parable tells us that we cannot control the first arrow. It will hit its mark and cause us some amount of pain or suffering, but we ourselves fire the second arrow. Through the practice of mindfulness we can learn to notice when the effect of the first arrow is beginning to turn into the second arrow and also learn to treat ourselves with forgiveness, kindness and compassion so that we do not create more needless suffering for ourselves.

Mindfulness Practices

Here we describe some of the most common and useful mindfulness practices which can suit a variety of aims and temperaments. There are many free resources out there for anyone who is interested in learning more about mindfulness or specific exercises, so we will not go into great detail here. We will instead describe each exercise so that you can get started right away, but should you need more explanation you can always look up the practice online.

Everyday Mindfulness – STOP/LEAF

This first exercise highlights the fact that mindfulness does not have to be a time-consuming, obscure practice, but instead should start to become part of everyday life in various ways. STOP and LEAF are two acronyms that help to remind us to pause what we are doing and, even if just for a moment, notice what is going on around us and within us.

STOP stands for:

Stop,
Take a breath,

Observe, and
Proceed.

LEAF stands for:

Look around,
Enjoy,
Appreciate what's around you, and
Familiarise yourself with your surroundings

While for some it can be difficult to create a regular, formal mindfulness practice, everyone can take advantage of this simple method that can provide numerous meaningful moments of mindfulness throughout a day. It really can be any time that you follow the STOP or LEAF process, but it can feel more meaningful to do so when in a natural, outdoor setting.

Mindful Breathing

The most common form of mindfulness practice is where you sit on a chair or the floor, eyes closed, with back straight and hands lightly resting on your lap and you use your breath as an anchor for your attention. That could be the sensation of your breath flowing through your nostrils, the rising and falling of your chest, or a general awareness of how it feels to breathe right this moment. You should set a timer for 5 or 10 minutes at first, and then try for longer sessions when you feel like it.

With this as your focus for the practice, the goal is not to keep perfect attention on your breath but rather to notice when your mind wanders and gently bring it back to the breath again. This process of being distracted and having to refocus will happen often, perhaps near constantly, and that is perfectly fine. In fact, it is precisely this process of frequently resetting your attention that you can think of like a bicep curl for your brain, strengthening your 'attention muscle' a little bit at a time.

You will likely notice that even though you want to keep focused on your breath, your mind will want to lead you off in all manner of directions – reflecting on the exercise itself, worrying about friends, thinking about your dinner tonight, making plans for your retirement in 50 years' time – which is entirely natural and largely unavoidable. Even experienced meditators still experience this kind of racing mind that never quite settles. The point is not to silence the mind, but to become aware of what is happening in it with curiosity and without judgement. It so happens that as you practice more, becoming increasingly able to detach from the flowing thoughts and emotions, letting them pass by instead of identifying with them, you will find yourself more often in a calmer state of mind.

Sometimes through this simple technique you can enter a flow-like state, where time fades away and you have no idea how long you have been sitting for. An hour-long meditation can feel like it has taken just 20 minutes. This is undoubtedly a pleasurable experience, but it is not the goal of mindfulness meditation. Any session where you *try* to stay present and aware with your experience is a success. In fact there is no way to fail at mindfulness, though if you fall asleep then you will not be getting any of the benefits of the practice, so it is best to try and avoid that!

Effective Calming – The Mindful Minute

You can use a similar technique to the one described earlier in order to settle nerves or anxiety before a big match or job interview for example.

Close your eyes and take three deep breaths in and out through your nose, breathing deep into your stomach so you can feel your stomach expanding and contracting. Start paying attention to the feeling of your breath entering your body and filling up your lungs, and then as you exhale notice where in your body you can sense the deflation. Continue to take 7 to 10 normal breaths and stay attentive to the changing sensations in your body as you breathe. Open your eyes and take a few seconds to notice how you feel.

This method incorporates a deep breathing technique with a focusing of the mind, which together can quickly bring you into a calmer, less anxious state.

The Body Scan

Instead of maintaining your focus on one thing, such as the feeling of your breath in your nostrils, a mindful body scan is where you shift your focus like a laser beam over different parts of your body, holding it in each place for some amount of time before moving on. It can be helpful to be guided through this exercise, and there are plenty of options to be found online, but it is also fine to do it without a guide. Ideally you should lie down, with eyes closed, arms resting by your sides. Start by taking a few deeper breaths, bringing your awareness to the feelings associated with breathing. Then when you are ready you can shift your attention to a body part, for example your left foot. Imagine your attention is that laser beam, focusing its full power on precisely that foot. Notice what sensations are there – contact with the floor, temperature, discomfort, tingling – and if there are no discernible sensations then you can just notice that. Try to be present with whatever is there for you, without judgement, without thinking that anything is right or wrong. Discomfort or pain is to be treated with the same approach, without trying to correct your position or relieve the discomfort.

After a minute or so you can shift the laser beam to your left lower leg, noticing any new sensations there. Each time your attention wanders, gently bring it back to the body part without chastising yourself. Continue this process, spending some time on each body part through the upper left leg, right foot, lower right leg, upper right leg, pelvis region, stomach, chest, shoulders and neck, and then onto the face – chin, cheekbones, forehead, eyebrows, nose and lips – and finally the top of your head.

The whole exercise should take at least 10 to 15 minutes, but can be lengthened as much as you like. This is a particularly good exercise to practice after training sessions, and afterwards you will likely find yourself in a much more relaxed physical and mental state than when you started. The idea of imagining your attention as if it were a laser or spotlight, moving its beam around your body, can be very engaging. You begin to realise the power of attention, as a body part that filled your entire mind one second dissolves completely in the next as you shift focus to the next body part.

Process Mantras

Process mantras are particularly relevant to athletes, but can be adapted to any situation in life where you recognise that you could benefit from being more present and aware. These are effectively trigger words or short phrases which you choose in advance and connect to a specific situation or context and that reminds you to bring your focus back to where you want it to be.

Examples of process mantras:

- An ice hockey player giving themselves the mantra of 'fast and light' that they repeat to themselves right before every restart. This mantra is a reminder to be ready for when the puck drops but also incorporates some positive description of their best playing style.

- A marathon runner who sets an alarm to sound on their watch every 10 minutes, which triggers them to repeat their mantra 'born to run', connecting them to their passion for running instilled in them by their parents.

- A Judoka who is primed, in the final moments of a close fight, to run the phrase 'pressure is a privilege' through their mind, which gives them a glimpse of the attitude that they love the intensity of the sport, allowing them to perform with more freedom in the moment.

Given the importance of having the right focus at the right time in sport, integrating a strategy for making sure it will be there for you can be incredibly powerful. As any meditator will confirm, simply wanting to hold your concentration on something is not enough to keep it there. You need constant reminders or awareness-raisers to bring your mind back from whatever strange place it has wandered off to; the same goes for high-pressure moments in sport too. You can create a portfolio of process mantras for yourself that mean different things to you and are triggered at different times. It can take discipline and effort to become consistent in repeating them, but once they are automatically primed they can become one of the most powerful drivers of high performance.

My personal experience with mantras has shown me exactly this. I created a number of different mantras that I would use at specific moments during a fencing bout, such as when defending a big lead or in a sudden-death score situation. My most consistently used mantra, *'Now Fight'*, helped me stay focused and in touch with my optimal mindset and body language. The consistency of my performances skyrocketed when I introduced it to my game.

Imagine the effect on your confidence and your performance of knowing that your attention would be right where you wanted it at the most important moments.

Mindful Eating

With our busy lives today, it is all too easy to wolf our meals down without them ever touching the sides, and without taking the time to really savour or enjoy them. At your next meal try being more mindful about it. Try to take in more of the sensations, noticing the smells, textures and temperatures of the foods on your plate. Go a bit slower, taking time between each mouthful to appreciate them. This can be a combined mindfulness and gratitude exercise, as you raise your awareness of what there is to be appreciated, rather than rushing through a meal on autopilot.

You can also try a more focused mindful eating exercise, where you bring all your senses to the fore. Sit down with a raisin or a piece of candy and place it on the palm of your hand. First you are going to inspect it visibly with all the curiosity of someone who has never in their life seen such a thing. Look at it right up close and try to notice every line, reflection, texture and shape that it holds. Spend a good few minutes on this part. Then get a feel for it between your fingers, noticing how hard or soft it is and anything else about its physical form. Next you can smell it, trying to really attend to it as if for the first time. Then you can place it on your tongue, but without sucking or eating it. Notice the first taste of it when it touches your tongue, and whether that taste changes after some seconds. You can also notice your thoughts about the exercise, or whether you feel the urge to just bite into it. Finally, you can start chewing, almost in slow motion and deliberately, tuning in to the new tastes and sensations in your mouth with each chew, swallowing after a while when it feels natural.

You can repeat the exercise with another piece of the same food, trying to attend to different inputs from your senses. The point of this exercise is to tune your awareness to the hundreds of small things that you miss out on noticing when going at normal speed through life. Slowing down to take in more of the sights, smells and tastes can open up a new world of awareness and appreciation for the simple things.

7   The Athlete Identity

MORE THAN AN ATHLETE

— LEBRON JAMES' T-SHIRT

Competitive athletes of all ages will have a certain degree of athletic identity: that is, a sense of themselves that relates to being an athlete. Professional athletes will likely have quite a strong athletic identity since it is their profession and they have dedicated their lives to it.

Having a strong athletic identity has clear advantages, including a commitment to training, the ability to focus on sport-related goals, as well as heightened motivation and discipline. But there are associated dangers when an athlete's athletic identity becomes too dominant, when they see no side to themselves other than as an athlete.

If an athlete has an exclusive athletic identity, their entire sense of self and self-esteem comes from being an athlete. Consequently, when their athletic career is not going so well (as every athlete will experience at some point) or they are injured or unable to train and compete for any reason, then they will experience a drop in self-esteem, are more likely to suffer from depression and can even experience an identity crisis. The Canadian, eight-time Winter X Games Ski Slopestyle champion Kaya Turski had a nightmare lead up to the 2014 Sochi

Winter Olympics. She first ruptured her ACL, requiring extensive reconstruction and rehabilitation. Then, having recovered in miraculous time to claim her place on the start line of the Olympics, she caught a virus on the way to the Games, and *then* dislocated her shoulder in her first qualification run of the event. She did not qualify for the finals for the first time in her athletic career. She described the dark period that followed:

> For the first 25 years of my life, I saw my value as a person directly linked to my success in sport, fed by big-time wins. And although I had been working on redefining that very notion, I hadn't yet been forced to live it. In the months after the Olympics, I sunk into a depression, withdrawing from others and barely leaving the house. … It took me almost two years to forgive myself for not having overcome what I now recognize to be very difficult circumstances.

Identity crisis is a common experience among retiring or transitioning athletes, which is in large part due to an overly dominant athletic identity.

Dr Kitrina Douglas was a pro golfer for 20 years before she turned her attention to academic research, notably into the experiences and mental health of athletes. In a study of female pro golfers, Douglas discovered three distinct personal narratives relating to the sporting life stories of these athletes who had made it to the highest level of their sport. The first was the traditionally dominant *performance narrative*, where competition, winning and gaining social esteem were critical elements. The second was a *discovery narrative*, where the athletes were most concerned with discovering, experiencing and exploring life in a full and multidimensional sense. And finally, the *relational narrative*, where the emphasis was on the interpersonal relationship with others, such as a parent, rather than a focus on the self. Douglas presents the evidence that a too heavy reliance on a single, performance narrative can be troublesome when the person's experience no longer fits with their narrative. According to Douglas, 'Retirement and serious injury are two moments when an athlete may struggle to reconcile or make sense of the dramatic changes occurring within her life.' She explains that for one of the participants in the study who exemplified this singular perspective 'both poor performance and prospective retirement are described in terms of narrative wreckage. When things do not go well in performance terms (for instance poor play leading to being eliminated from a tournament), the outcome is personal shame and a loss of self-esteem. When this athlete contemplates retirement as "like losing a limb", she hints at problems to come when she is no longer able to maintain her sense of self through winning golf tournaments.' In this study, the discovery narrative is presented as a far more stable and healthy approach to sport, where the performance and the person are not inextricably entwined.

Benjamin Houltberg and his colleagues also investigated the effect of differing identity narratives in elite athletes in the United States. Their findings corroborated Douglas' study, showing that athletes with a strong *performance-based narrative identity* demonstrated the highest levels of depression, anxiety and shame and the lowest levels of life satisfaction, whereas athletes with a *purpose-based narrative identity* had the highest levels of psychological well-being across those same parameters.

It is essential, therefore, to cultivate both a multifaceted identity narrative within sport – comprising aspects related to performance, purpose and discovery – as well as elements of yourself which relate to things outside of your sporting world that have real, personal value. These can include relationships with family, friends or a partner; study; part-time work or volunteering; and creative interests, such as art, music or reading

– anything you like that will add to and increase the richness of your sense of self-worth.

Take a moment to think about your own sporting narrative. Where do you derive the most motivation and most meaning? If you recognise that it is dominated by performance aspects, then consider how you might open it up to draw on a broader sense of meaning and opportunities to feel fulfilment in your sporting life.

Returning to the example we discussed earlier, of Marcus Rashford forcing policy change at the national level, the catalyst for his campaigning came during an extended period of injury. He elaborates: 'the injury prevented me from doing pretty much anything, so I needed to set my mind on something that would turn a negative into a positive and help those who needed it most. I've always had a wish to give back to the community that got me to where I am today but the football schedule had never really allowed me to focus on what I wanted to do and how best to go about it.'

Rashford's desire to give back to his community provided the route through which he could turn the negative of his injury into a positive. No one could have imagined just how impactful that decision would turn out to be. If Rashford had accepted the all-too-common attitude that athletes should just stick to sports, there would likely be 1.3 million more children going hungry in the UK during school holidays.

We must get past the idea that athletes often just have no time or energy for other pursuits. That stance creates acceptance for the development of athletes with single-dimensional identities, leading to inevitable internal trouble.

Instead, we must cultivate the understanding that more rounded and grounded athletes will stay in the sport longer and perform better. Having valued aspects of their lives that are wholly independent of their sporting world can give an athlete confidence and a sense of perspective when they are performing, as well as an essential refuge when things go wrong. This works both ways, so when there is tension at work or in their family, an athlete can find refuge and stress relief from their sport. Lizzie Simmonds, 13-time British swimming champion and 2-time Olympian, writes an online blog to reflect on her own experience and offer help to others on their path.

> *You are an athlete. That identity will define many of the decisions you make on a daily basis, and your purpose will be driven by acting in accordance with this. There is a good chance that it will be the strongest driving force you will feel each day. You'll have goals, targets and objectives that give you vision, but you will also rely on your identity to help you push through when things get tough. This is a huge part of sport, and adopting this all-encompassing identity is part of what makes you great at what you do.*
>
> *But it isn't everything.*
>
> *Although you may not recognise it at the time, you are much more than you think, beyond your performance on the pitch, field, track etc. Even though sport may occupy most of your waking thoughts and actions, you don't have to limit yourself to a singular existence. So, ask yourself what are the other components that make you, well, you?*

The important thing is that your identity should be *multidimensional*, with all the added richness, safe refuge and uplift that come from having many things to care about in life.

Knowing Your Core Values and How to Live Them

Your beliefs become your thoughts,
Your thoughts become your words,
Your words become your actions,
Your actions become your habits,
Your habits become your values,
Your values become your destiny.

— GANDHI

It is our 'why' that really drives us in everything we do and can give a sense of connectedness and meaning to all areas of life. This links closely with Viktor Frankl's story of recognising purpose in life as the deciding factor in surviving the worst possible circumstances.

Simon Sinek took the business world by storm with his best-selling book, *Start with Why*. It brought Frankl's revelation about purpose into popular culture with the simple, yet inspiring message: '*Most of us live our lives by accident – we live as it happens. Fulfilment comes when we live our lives on purpose.* Once you discover your WHY, you are better able to align your beliefs with every choice and action you take, in order to find greater fulfilment in all that you do.'

It is clear that exploring your 'why' can have a profound effect. Getting enhanced clarity on what you value most about yourself can be an incredibly powerful tool for achieving your goals. It can help with motivation, direction and with maintaining a healthy perspective around your performances.

When you have a description of what you value about sport and about yourself when you play sport, it gives you a powerful sense that you are doing this because this is who you are or this is who you want to be, not because your coach or parent says you should do it. It can start to guide your behaviour because you have a clear vision of your best self, the one you want to live up to, and it provides a kind of mirror to hold up so you can notice when you are not doing that.

All of this comes down to living up to the values that matter the most to you, as consistently as possible – being the best version of yourself as much of the time as possible. Sport provides plenty of opportunities to be challenged in your choices, to try and lead you away from your best you. Can you live according to what you value, to your best you, or do you follow another, easier yet less fruitful path? This is the beauty and challenge of being values-led.

Here are some of the key advantages of working with deepening this understanding:

- Highlights the potential for the strengthening and development of your personal values through your chosen sport. *It is not just about getting the best results but also about focused personal development*
- Gives an understanding that the true self is not affected by winning or losing, thereby providing increased freedom from the stress of competition
- Allows for greater integrity, ensuring there are common threads throughout your sporting and non-sporting lives.

In order to work on this, you will first need to establish your core values and then identify and explore how you can embody those values in life. We will describe here a process that can help you find your core values, and then provide some reflective exercises that will bring them to life and give them practical application.

The process for choosing your values is as follows:

Step 1. Start with a broad, open-ended thought experiment.
Step 2. Consider and answer some specific, probing questions.
Step 3. Select your values with the help of a comprehensive list.

Step 1. The Thought Experiment

This is essentially a twist on a visualisation exercise you might have heard of, where you imagine what someone would say at your funeral. But instead of a funeral, you should imagine that you are at the end of a long, illustrious sports career, having achieved everything you could have wanted along the way. A reception is being held in your honour and two people will stand up and give a speech about you. The first thing you have to decide is who those speakers would be; choose one from your sporting life and the other from your non-sporting life, so as to provide a more rounded picture of you as a person and not just the athletic you.

Now try and imagine what you would most want those people to say about you, making notes as you go. Of course the speakers would be saying amazing, flattering things, but what specifically would those be? They might start with 'Olympic and World Champion, G.O.A.T. ... etc.' but that list of accolades is not the part we are interested in here. What do they say about how and why you were so great? What did you show along the way to make you so revered and respected as an athlete and as a person? The non-sporting speaker would likely say things about you as a person, a friend, about your history together and relationship, whereas the sporting speaker would likely talk about you as an athlete, a teammate, the traits that made you a great performer and leader.

If you become stuck you could also think about what you would not want said about you. For example, for some the idea of being known as 100 per cent focused on their sporting goals would be a great thing, whereas others might prefer to be known for all the great things they did aside from their sporting career.

Through the statements you imagine being spoken, you may start to get a sense of what you care about most, what you want to be remembered for and, therefore, how you most want to go about achieving your goals starting now.

Step 2. Probing Questions

Now you can try to answer some questions designed to get you to think a bit more specifically about what you value about yourself and others:

- What aspects of your personality do you like the most?
- What would your friends say that they liked most about you?
- What aspects of personality do you most admire in other people you respect?
- Who are your sporting heroes? What is it about them as people and as athletes that you admire or respect, apart from their achievements and skills?

If you haven't ever considered questions like this before, it might not be easy to come up with all the answers on the spot. Going through this process can be an eye-opening exercise for those who have not thought deeply about it before, so it is worth giving yourself time to consider it, and maybe come back to the questions with time to reflect in between.

Step 3. Choose Your Values

With the help of the values list at the end of this book, you can now start to pinpoint the specific core values that you want to start integrating more into your life. It is worth pointing out that there are a great many values that are highly attractive to every individual. Through this process you will be narrowing down the list of appreciated values to those you consider most essential. This is important because these core values will be used to help guide your behaviour and choices and if there are too many of them, they can point in too many different directions and the process becomes too complex and slow.

So, keeping in mind the statements and answers that arose in steps 1 and 2, read through the list of values and start by making a long list of all those values that most resonate with you, perhaps with a maximum of around 15 to 20.

Then pulling your long list aside, you should read through the list and narrow it down to the 10 that are most important to you.

The next step is to pick out five or six from here that you want to keep. Looking closely at your list of 10 you may find that some of the values relate closely to each other, and perhaps can be merged together. The important thing to remember here is that this is *your* list and values themselves are not simple, concrete things. You can imbue a value with the meaning that you want it to have. For example, if you have chosen two values – 'being of service' and 'kindness', you could decide that for you kindness holds within it being of service, because giving back is an expression of what you understand as kindness. Similarly, the value 'persistence' could feasibly hold within it the ideas of passion, hard work, resilience and ambition, among various other qualities. However, you should try not to stretch too far when combining values together like this; it should only be done if one value truly expresses for you an integral aspect of another.

This shortlist of five or six values can be considered your core values, but there is one more selection to make. Six is still too many to really focus your attention and guide you when it counts, so you are going to highlight three of them as your higher core values. These are the ones you will consult first and that will take precedence whenever there is conflict between your core values.

It is important to know that these values represent a snapshot in time in your life, and you should not consider them as carved in stone to follow you to your grave. It is far better to take this as a good starting point and know that you can always reassess your choices at any time (and indeed you should come back to this process once or twice a year to check if they still feel right). A person's values will naturally change over time and also differ according to the aspect of their identity that is under consideration. What is most important to you in your role as an athlete will likely not be the same as in your role as a student or employee, as a son/daughter or husband/wife. When I went through this process in my role as Performance Director, my values had shifted subtly since the time I did it as an athlete. The newly included values represented the different aspects of my character that I needed to shine through in this period of my life.

So, you have selected your five or six core values and highlighted which three are higher core values. The first thing to do is to write these on a piece of paper or cards and then stick them up in your room, carry them in your kit bag or make them your background for your devices – anything to make sure they remain visible to you on a daily basis.

Now you can use the following exercises to make these values more practical in your life in sport and beyond.

For each of your core values, make a list of all the ways that value could be expressed, developed or strengthened in your sporting life. *Your sporting life consists not only of competition and training, but also of the travelling, social time with teammates and coaches, interacting with younger and older athletes and everything else that you experience in the name of sport.*

Some values have a natural connection to the performance environment, such as being *fearless*. Others might not be quite so easily performance-oriented, such as being *caring*. But there are still clear ways this could be expressed in a sporting context:

- Looking after the new players/members of the club/ team
- Checking in with teammates when they seem to be having a rough time
- Not using harsh or unpleasant language to avoid offending people
- Having self-compassion to forgive and begin again after disappointment

Think ahead to what is about to come up in your sporting life and identify times when you may be able to express your values through your behaviour. Consider especially those situations where you may be under the most pressure or more challenged, as these are the moments when you are most likely to lose connection to your values-led path.

Reflect on the day or week just gone. Were there any times when your behaviour did not match up to your core values? Consider how you felt immediately afterwards. Thinking about it, how do you feel now? How would you like to act differently the next time a similar situation arises?

Through this process you will begin to see that there is much more to be gained from your sporting life than just improved technique and silverware. You now have specific techniques to develop the characteristics and personality traits that you value most about yourself. You now have a compilation of small *why's* and one large one – personal growth – which are in no way reliant on sporting results.

Embrace Vulnerability

To dare is to lose one's footing momentarily. Not to dare is to lose oneself.

— Søren Kierkegaard

There is an adverse performance behaviour which is particularly prevalent among young athletes. The phenomenon can be seen playing out in tournaments and in practices of every sport, in every country. It may be hard to notice at first, but coaches and spectators will soon pick up on it. The athlete they are watching just doesn't seem to be giving their fullest effort. It is not that they're being outplayed, nor that they're making mistakes. It seems as if they are purposefully holding back. They are losing without ever really trying. Understandably, this can be incredibly frustrating to witness from the sidelines.

What can possibly be going on? How can an otherwise motivated, ambitious athlete put in a thoroughly sub-standard performance and even lose a match, without having once tried to find a higher gear?

At the heart of the issue is vulnerability. And the answer to this conundrum can be found by unravelling the profound misconceptions that we tend to maintain around this word. But first, what exactly is vulnerability and what is it not?

Traditionally we equate vulnerability with weakness. We imagine an animal vulnerable to attack, and therefore open to being wounded. But while it is true that being vulnerable involves a certain kind of openness, physically or more often psychologically, it doesn't follow that vulnerability is equal to weakness. In fact, embracing vulnerability shows inner strength and integrity. It is courage, it is being brave.

This is the misconception that we must address generally but especially in sport culture, if we are to unleash more of our athletes' potentials. Let's unpack the contradiction.

The preeminent vulnerability researcher Brené Brown wrote the groundbreaking book *The Power of Vulnerability: Teachings on Authenticity, Connection and Courage*, as well as giving one of the most watched TED talks of all time, titled 'The Power of Vulnerability'. Brown describes vulnerability as the feeling we get during times of uncertainty, risk or emotional exposure. If you consider a performance of any kind – sport, art, business – each one involves one or more of these elements. Indeed, all sporting performances inherently involve uncertainty, as the result is, by definition, unknown. This uncertainty in turn often produces a sense of emotional exposure for the participants who care deeply about that result. And emotional exposure then represents a risk to the ego, as it faces the potential backlash from mistakes or failure.

Now consider the athlete in question, holding back from giving their all in a match. In light of this description of vulnerability, it begins to make perfect sense. The ego is trying to protect itself from the risk of an uncertain, emotionally charged situation. If the athlete were to give absolutely everything to the performance and still lose or make mistakes, the emotional backlash could be severe. So instead they protect themselves by not really trying and therefore not putting any significant part of themselves on the line. Justifications after the fact often follow: 'I just didn't care enough' or 'I could see straight away I wasn't going to win' or 'I couldn't find the motivation to work hard'. These post-rationalisations, often unconscious, cover over the fact that the athlete simply was not willing to put themselves out there, not willing to be *vulnerable*.

And this is the key point – in order to perform at their best, athletes must embrace vulnerability. They must feel the uncertainty, the risk, of putting their emotions on the line and go out and give everything they have anyway. This is the definition of courage. In fact, courage is not the absence of fear; it is feeling afraid and doing the job anyway!

Everyone wants to be courageous, but few make the connection that to be courageous requires you to be vulnerable first. I would say that most young athletes have not fully understood or embraced that connection. So here is the contradiction laid bare – everyone wants to be courageous, but no one wants to be vulnerable. One does not come without the other, so if you want to reach your potential and meet pressure with courage, you must be prepared to seek out and embrace moments of vulnerability.

Without an understanding of the reality of vulnerability and courage you will forever be at the mercy of your changing mood and state of mind. Sometimes you will feel confident and able to risk more, and sometimes your ego will recoil from exposure and require greater self-protection.

We should also be teaching young athletes about *how* to be courageous. They must understand that it is not a question about being brave *or* afraid but that bravery is about feeling afraid, accepting that feeling and moving forward anyway.

We need to build awareness around feeling *uncomfortable* during a performance. Everyone has heard the message about 'getting out of your comfort zone' in order to make gains and develop; feeling uncomfortable in a situation is also a prerequisite for being courageous. We could aim to train an action trigger in athletes around that feeling of discomfort. So when the ego has noticed that there is a lot at stake and wants to put up a protective barrier, such as withholding effort, the athlete would instead be cued to see it as an opportunity for courage and step up their efforts. All too often this moment of discomfort goes unnoticed for what it truly is – an essential milestone for peak performance – and the reaction is hijacked by unwanted subconscious forces.

Embracing vulnerability also offers profound benefits beyond sporting performance. Brené Brown identifies vulnerability as the foundation of empathy, creativity, belonging and love. Certainly, if you cannot open yourself up to people, then love and belonging will elude you, and if you are not willing to risk failing then there is no hope of innovation or creativity.

As Brown puts it: 'If we want greater clarity in our purpose, or deeper and more meaningful lives, vulnerability is the path.'

When Brown asked people to finish the sentence 'Vulnerability is …', their answers exposed how critical the concept is and how central it is to so many of our most valuable emotions. Here are some of the responses:

Vulnerability is …

- standing up for myself.
- trying something new.
- asking for help.
- saying no.
- starting my own business.
- sharing something I wrote publicly.
- falling in love.
- saying, 'I love you' first.
- being accountable.
- asking for forgiveness.
- helping my wife with terminal cancer to write her will.

These responses could just as well be examples of courage. They show that vulnerability is implicit in taking responsibility, being honest, opening yourself up for great potential loss or gain and showing humanity. If the armour is up and you are protecting yourself from that uncomfortable, vulnerable feeling, then all of this is off the table to you.

We would all benefit from a better understanding of vulnerability. It would allow us to make far more of our individual and shared potential.

8   The Stoic Approach

The Controllables – Preparation, Effort, Attitude

> *The chief task in life is simply this: to identify and separate matters so that I can say clearly to myself which are externals not under my control, and which have to do with the choices I actually control. Where do I look for good and evil? Not to uncontrollable externals, but within myself to the choices that are my own ...*

— EPICTETUS

At the heart of Stoic philosophy is gaining clarity over what we can change and what we can't change in our lives. Those elements we can't control are not worth spending energy on; we must gather the full power of our attention and energy on what we can exert some control over. Note 'some control' is not the same as having total control over something. Even something as personal as your attitude will be affected by many things that are out of your control, such as your biological makeup, subconscious beliefs or local environment. But you can exert an element of conscious control over your attitude, and therefore it is appropriate to spend time working on it.

We propose using the framework of the three controllables – preparation, effort and attitude – in order to find greater clarity about what you should be focusing your energies on within a sporting context.

Preparation

An athlete is largely in control of many aspects of their preparation: punctuality and preparedness for training, studying tactics and doing performance analysis, their eating and sleeping patterns, using recovery time optimally, maintaining their equipment – the list goes on. It is clear that those athletes who prepare efficiently and professionally for competition give themselves the best chance of performing well, even when the conditions outside their control are not optimal. Athletes who prepare well experience fewer surprises in competition and are more ready to deal with obstacles placed in their way. They also get the priceless peace of mind that comes from knowing they had done everything they could to give themselves the best chance of success.

Since there is so much to consider within the sphere of preparation, there is no simple formula for optimising it. It is critical to draw on all the resources available to you, especially coaches, teammates, opponents and older athletes from your sport, as you consider each aspect of your preparation and how you can improve it. Areas to consider include:

- **Training**: How much? When? How intense?
- **Sleep**: How many hours per night? How deep? Habits around bedtime.
- **Diet**: What? How much? When?
- **Rest and recovery**: Get attuned to your body's needs, take it seriously and know your own boundaries.
- **Getting ready for an event/tournament**: Packing list, equipment maintenance, know the relevant information about event.

In my experience leading The True Athlete Projects' Mentoring Programme, this topic of preparation is always one which the younger mentees find incredibly beneficial to discuss with their mentors. Through discussion they quickly realise how much opportunity there is in optimising their routines, and the mentors have a wealth of knowledge to draw on to help guide them. Try to find ways to discuss the areas listed earlier with a mentor, coach or anyone with long experience in sport.

Effort and Attitude

When I rejoined the British fencing team in 2014 after a two-year break, our team was the strongest we had seen in many decades in Britain. We felt confident we could qualify for the Rio Olympics in 2016, but it would not be easy. In fact, it would require two firsts in British fencing history – the first time for a team to qualify via the world rankings, and the first time ever for a British team to rise above our fiercest rivals for the Olympic spot, Germany. There were also elements of the situation that could take qualification out of our hands, depending on how the other European nations fared. At the start of the year-long qualification process we gave ourselves at best a 50/50 chance. We knew that we would have to put our hearts and dreams on the line for a full, gruelling year of competitions; and we had only a 50 per cent chance of success. That was when our team psychologist, Danielle Norenberg, stepped in and presented us with another option – one which did not rely on us qualifying for the Olympics to be a success. The tool she taught us not only turned out to be ideal for dealing with the year-long pressure and uncertainty but also helped us achieve our mission – to overtake the Germans and qualify for Rio. That tool was the Effort & Attitude system (E&A).

Here we will consider effort and attitude within the context of a sporting performance, either in training or competition.

This section is more specific than the last and consists of two parts.

> **Part One:** Creating a description of your best effort and attitude during a performance
>
> **Part Two:** Introducing a rating system to assess your performance based only on the aspects included in your best effort and attitude descriptions, nothing else

This approach takes the focus entirely away from results and outcomes and places it firmly on the thing that will help you the most, namely the task at hand. This also provides a way to judge your performance based on the process and not just the outcome.

This approach has a number of powerful benefits:

1. It increases clarity about what your top performance actually looks and feels like.
2. Naturally it leads to a reduction in the stress around competing as you receive continued affirmation that the only things that will help you perform your best are all entirely within your control – there is no need to worry about anything else! Through specifically focusing on those aspects of performance you will find you are able to produce your top levels of effort and attitude more consistently.
3. It enables greater understanding of confidence as just a feeling like any other, and that you can create that feeling by starting with confident *actions*.

Effort

In order to help you create a description of your best effort, you need to think back on some of your best performances. You should try to describe those performances in a way that any onlooker would be able to recognise if they had your description to hand. We are not interested in the technical, tactical or mental here, but rather in the more physical elements of those performances. What was your body position? In what way and how much did you move? For example, a badminton player might list *high hand*, *deep crouch* and *light feet* in their best effort description.

Another way to think about this is: How do you look and behave when you are at your most confident? What kind of actions do you take? The badminton player might think that they do best when they show their readiness for the start of every point by adopting an aggressive posture while seeking to take up space on the court.

Different sports require effort in different ways, but every athlete should be able to describe what their best effort looks like with a little … effort. It can help to think of the opposite – what happens when things don't feel good, when motivation is low? What is the physical evidence of a low effort level? Here, the badminton player might point to sloppier body language or heavier landing of their feet when stretching to play shots.

What you're looking for here is to get down on paper roughly three to seven points that describe different aspects of your effort. They should all be things that you have some control over regardless of environmental conditions, opponent, referee or any other external factor.

It does not have to be an exhaustive list and can easily be added to and updated. Indeed this list should naturally evolve over time as you develop your skills and your game matures. The key is that these are things that you know help you to perform better *and* that you have influence over.

Once you have a list you are happy with, you can move on to part two: attitude.

Attitude

This is the mental side of the coin, but mostly in terms of mindset rather than mental skills. Using the same process as before you should try to describe the kind of mindset you have when you are performing at your best. Are you all fired up, or cool, calm and collected? Are you serious or playful? Do you react to unforeseen situations by giving vent to your emotions, or do you let them slip off you like water off a duck's back? Our hypothetical badminton player might decide that they want a warrior-type mindset, where they show no fear, will never give up and will take challenges and bad luck in their stride.

It might not always feel that you are in control of the various aspects of attitude, such as your level of arousal, but given the right tools no one and nothing can stop you from forming the mindset that you want.

It can also be helpful to think about your desired ideal attitude even if you have not yet managed to achieve it – that way, you can use it as a target. Perhaps you look up to someone in your sport because of how they deal with setbacks, or someone who plays with constant, evident determination.

Again, for the purpose of this exercise, it can help to think about examples of your mindset when things have not gone well, to help identify the signs that show when you have not got the attitude that you want.

Here you should be looking for at least two to three points that describe your best attitude.

Together with the 'best effort' statements described earlier, it may be useful to put these onto cue cards that you can look at periodically throughout the day, during a training session, or in competition.

Frances Houghton, five-time British Olympic rower, winning three silver medals, described her own distillation of effort and attitude in her book, *Learnings from Five Olympic Games*:

> *Too much technical detail would scramble my brain, so I would boil everything down to three points on the back of my hand – never more than three, and always in the order I would do them from the green light. For example: (1) legs first, (2) hips over, (3) loose.*

Part Two: The Rating System

Having described your top-level effort and best possible attitude (or at least a good starting point) you can now consider using a rating system as a way of continuously and powerfully working with them.

The essence and strength of the rating system is that it provides a method to analyse your performance purely in relation to how well you have lived up to your E&A descriptions. This is akin to rating each day in your life based on how well you lived up to your values.

After each performance (training or competition) you rate yourself on a scale of 0 to 5.

- '0' being not matching up to your E&A descriptions in any sense at all.
- '5' being nailing everything on the list to the best of your ability.

It is very important, but also quite difficult in the beginning, to try to ignore the result or outcome when coming up with your score. This means that you could lose heavily and still have given a 5/5 E&A performance, but equally you could win easily and only rate yourself as 2/5. This knowledge offers a sense of freedom from the shackles of result-orientation that can have a profound positive impact on your performances.

This is not the end of the process, however. The questions that follow are perhaps more important than the rating itself. The order of questioning goes:

1. What is my score?
2. What made it more than a '3' and why wasn't it quite a '5'? (for the case of a rating of '4' in response to the first question)
3. What do I need to do to improve my score by at least one point next time (or maintain it, in the case of a 5/5)?

This process of questioning can happen in your head or it can be led by a coach, teammate or anyone else. It can be done *hot* (during or immediately after matches/performances) or *cold* (some time after the event). As well as focusing your attention on the most important aspects of your performance, it has the added benefit of drawing you into a more analytical frame of mind as you try to access the information you need to answer the questions. This is especially helpful when you are caught up in the emotion and pressure of competition.

Consider sharing this method with someone who will be present with you during training or competition, such as a coach or teammate, who can challenge you in the moment to answer these questions. It also helps if they know your E&A descriptions, to be able to give feedback based on what they see.

This approach does not replace technical and tactical feedback and analysis, but rather is meant to complement them. This method of reflection is especially powerful in the case of repeated performances, where an athlete has time to reflect before their next performance, such as field athletes who get multiple attempts.

Over time, using the strategies described here, you will find that your mind begins to naturally focus on your own effort and attitude, and is far less easily distracted by events outside your control. Since the only important assessment is your own E&A rating, you start to ask yourself: 'What point is there expending energy on things that don't really influence my performance?'

The closest thing an athlete has to a superpower is the ability to focus on the task at hand, and the ability to influence it without being distracted. The E&A rating system is a key tool to achieving that.

Acceptance and Defusion

To all you athletes who fight, sweat and struggle every day in the pursuit of what truly matters to you. You have hopes and dreams, and doubts that you will ever reach them.
So very human. So very right.
—Jacob Hansen, Christoffer Henriksen
and Carsten Hvid Larsen

Acceptance

There has been a relatively recent but significant shift in sport psychology when it comes to helping performers deal with their unhelpful thoughts and emotions. The shift moves away from the confrontational approach, where athletes are encouraged to use their inner dialogue to respond logically to distracting thoughts, and towards an approach of accepting the full range of thoughts and emotions that can arise as a natural part of the experience of being an athlete.

The sport psychology department at Team Danmark, the Danish elite sport organisation, is among those leading the way in this approach. In 2017 Team Danmark convened the first-ever International Summit on Mindfulness and Acceptance Approaches in Elite Sport, led by the three prominent Danish sport psychologists to whom the previous epigraph is attributed. The summit was attended by 48 of the world's top sport psychology practitioners across 17 countries, showing the broad appetite for this new approach. An approach based on acceptance, the three psychologists propose, means dropping the struggle against the full range of thoughts and feelings which are such a natural part of sport and life – giving the athlete some breathing space and letting them just be there, without getting overwhelmed.

This shift in approach can be illustrated by the vivid image of being in a tug of war against an elephant, where the elephant represents your subconscious mind. Trying to pull the elephant into line with how you want your mind to be working is an exhausting and essentially fruitless task, but if instead you let the rope drop, then the elephant no longer has any power over you. It is still there, of course, but you have far more flexibility to choose what to focus your energies on.

There is a common misconception among athletes that in order to perform to your best you need to get rid of the negative thoughts and feelings and be in a totally positive and calm place of mind. This idea suggests that feeling underconfident or nervous before a competition indicates that things are going to go badly. We look up to the best athletes in the world, we see their uber-confident demeanour and assume that they have none of the same worries or doubts as we do. All of this is misleading. Everyone has doubts and fears. Those feelings do not have to negatively impact a performance, and the trick that the very best performers have mastered is how to feel those things and *perform anyway*! A story from my own experience illustrates this point as well as any other I can think of. In the athlete warm-up area of the fencing stadium at the 2016 Rio Olympics I happened to visit the toilet at a time when one of my competitors was being violently sick in the stall next to mine. As I washed my hands one of the Italian fencers emerged from the toilet looking white as a sheet. I thought, '*Poor guy, must have gotten food poisoning or something, right on the day of his Olympic event.*' That poor guy then went on to win the gold medal, his first ever victory in a major event. It must have been a monumental bout of nerves that caused his sickness that morning, and yet, he was able to carry on and produce his life-time best performance regardless.

Competing in something you care about inherently triggers strong emotions, and the thoughts that arise are based on deep, biological processes concerning threat to the ego. It is not worth engaging in battle with such deep and powerful forces. Instead, you approach situations ready to accept whatever thoughts or emotions arise; but that is the start, not the end of the process. Acceptance buys you mental space, freed from the struggle with the elephant, and allows you to direct your attention to what is most important. In sport, that is a commitment to the actions and values that will help you play to your best (see the sections on values in chapter 7, and 'The Controllables' in this chapter).

Acceptance is not the same as being resigned to your fate. Its literal meaning is *taking what has been offered*. British sport and exercise psychologist Jenna Woolven describes it as like receiving a disappointing Christmas present from your grandma and opening it in front of the whole family. Instead of getting upset, making a scene and confronting your granny about it, you politely say '*thank you*' and carry on playing with the presents that you like more. The same goes for the unwanted thoughts and feelings that your mind offers you. Instead of causing a bigger scene by worrying about them, confronting them, trying to push them away, you simply accept them, leave them aside and move your focus back to where you want it to be.

Defusion

Defusion is a method that can help to underpin an attitude of acceptance. It describes the ability of stepping back and detaching somewhat from the thoughts and feelings going through your mind. The opposite of defusion is becoming enshrouded and lost in rumination and self-judgement triggered by your thoughts and feelings. It is natural for troublesome, illogical thoughts to arrive during moments of high pressure, such as '*I'm going to lose*' or '*I must perform perfectly or it's not worth it*'. If an athlete identifies, or *fuses,* too much with such thoughts it is likely to be detrimental to their performance. In the previous examples it could dent their confidence or pressure them to take a less risky and ultimately less effective path.

Defusion can be trained effectively through mindfulness practice, which you have already learned in chapter 6; it allows you to notice the goings-on in your mind without attaching yourself to them. You learn to watch your thoughts go by like clouds floating past the window.

One strategy to help with defusion is to name or categorise thoughts as they arise. For instance:

- Worrying about the future
- Ruminating on the past
- Self-criticism

These processes automatically put you in the position of the observer, watching your thoughts and putting them in pigeonholes, providing just enough of a detachment to remove their effects.

Another method you can try is that when you notice a thought or feeling arise, instead of saying to yourself '*I am nervous*', say instead '*I am an athlete having the thought – I am nervous*'. This language highlights that you *are not* the thought, you are the athlete or indeed the person, and you are merely experiencing a thought. This is a key distinction here, where we all too often get so wrapped up in our thoughts and feelings that we come to believe that they define us, when in fact they do no such thing. Anyone who has tried mindfulness practice even briefly can attest that the mind constantly throws us thoughts and emotions that we neither want nor choose. This approach is closely linked with the concept of *distanced self-talk* – using your own name and talking to yourself as you would to others. Ethan Kross, Professor of Psychology at the University of Michigan and author of *Chatter: The Voice in Our Head, Why It Matters and How to Harness It*, proposes that addressing yourself by your own name when considering problems in your life can help you think less emotionally and more wisely and therefore help you perform better under stress. So, for example, at times when I was particularly nervous right before a big match I might say to myself something along the lines of – '*Okay Laurence, this is what you are here for. Remember you love this intensity and you would rather be here than anywhere else right now. Time to go to work!*'

Defusion and acceptance allow us to reduce the tension that arises from an unhelpful inner dialogue, leaving us free to choose our response as we are no longer locked in to any automatic, emotional reaction. Such freedom and flexibility lay the foundation for resilience, as the negative thoughts and emotions are given less purchase in our minds and wreak far less havoc as a consequence. We are left able to focus our attention on what is helpful to us.

Gratitude

Gratitude is not only the greatest of the virtues, but the parent of all the others.

— CICERO

Gratitude is, simply put, noticing and appreciating the positive in life. It has deep roots within human evolutionary history, being connected to the value derived from helping and being helped by others in your tribe. It can be experienced as a general disposition, as an emotion, or in a behavioural sense, in the *act* of giving thanks. Gratitude implies humility, recognising that we could not have arrived where we are and achieved what we have without the contributions of those around us and those who came before us.

High performance sport has traditionally treated the concept of gratitude as soft or weak, but more recently it has – much like self-compassion – been proven to be a profound source of resilience and well-being. Gratitude has also been linked to a whole catalogue of positive psychological, physical and social indicators, including optimism, life satisfaction, sleep quality, social connectedness and altruistic behaviour. These links can become even stronger when the feeling of gratitude is acted upon and expressed outwardly.

Teri Mckeever, head coach of the women's swimming team at the University of California and former US Olympic swim coach, introduces gratitude practices with her squads. She believes the simple exercises transformed the energy of the athletes. Before certain training sessions she hands out pen and paper to her swimmers and asks them to write down 10 things that they are grateful for, before reading their list aloud to the group.

Mckeever says, 'The athletes like it because after they've had a hard day, they get to take a moment and think about what they're grateful for, and also hear teammates express that. The practices are always more productive, cohesive, and enjoyable for all of us.'

It is clear, then, that many of the qualities we've been conditioned to view as 'soft' can in fact provide us with a strong, resilient foundation from which to build a fulfilling life. They give us a sense of connectedness, both to others and the natural world around us.

In a performance setting, gratitude can be used to create a more positive, creative and calm mindset. Negative emotions such as stress and anxiety, which are common within athletic performance, have the effect of narrowing our focus. This dynamic has biological roots, as feeling fear or anxiety would enable our ancestors to marshal their full attention and energy towards the object of their fear. In an athletic performance these same emotions can become debilitating, reducing our ability to think rationally and adapt appropriately. An athlete who is suffering with excessive anxiety moments before their performance could think of what they have to be grateful for in that moment. This could be that they have been selected to represent their club or country; that they are fit and healthy and able to compete; that they get this chance to really test themselves and see what they are capable of; that they have good friends by their side … the list of possibilities is endless. The effect of thinking in this way is like a magic spell that counteracts the narrowing, debilitating aspect of their anxiety and can create the space to access a broader perspective, seeing the positives of their situation with greater clarity. The reality is that they are in no real danger, certainly not of the kind that made the negative emotions useful to our ancestors thousands of years ago. They are about to play a game which they are passionate about, and only their ego is being threatened. Remembering what they are grateful for will help them feel challenged instead of threatened, and will allow them to perceive their nerves as excitement for the opportunity ahead of them. The mantra mentioned earlier in the book, *pressure is a privilege*, leads to precisely that kind of switch of mindset.

This change of perspective can be summed up nicely as the 'got to' – 'get to' switch. Instead of thinking, '*I've got to go out and perform in front of all those people*', you can make the subtle but powerful change to '*I get to go out and perform in front of all those people*'. If you can do this, your mind will both consciously and subconsciously process the positives that underlie this statement. Flicking this mental switch can be effective in all areas of sport and life. Consider for a moment the implications and psychological benefits of changing 'got to' for 'get to' in these statements:

- I've got to go training again today.
- I've got to go see the physio about my injury.
- I've got to travel to another away game this weekend.
- I've got to combine a busy school schedule with my training.
- I've got to go shopping with my mum and sister.

This mental technique allows you to see the positives of a situation which might otherwise seem negative. One example of this from my own life comes every night when I put my toddler daughter to bed. She will not fall asleep without holding my hand throughout, and it can take anywhere from five minutes to over an hour for that to happen. It can easily become quite frustrating to have my evening disappear in the dark of her bedroom, but as soon as I make the 'get to' switch in mind, any frustration melts away. Like a blindfold pulled away from my eyes, suddenly I recognise that it allows me time to myself, without anywhere else to be or anything else to do. I can meditate, plan, ponder. And I get to hold my tired daughter's hand and help her get some much-needed sleep!

Even though athletes make a regular commitment to continue their sport and many know deep down that they love doing it, they can still be led by their brains into experiencing highly incongruent moments. Mathew Pinsent is one of Great Britain's greatest ever rowers, having won 10 world championship titles and gold medals in four consecutive Olympics between 1992 and 2004. Pinsent has spoken of his memory of being in a minibus on his way to one of those Olympic finals and praying that it would crash. As supreme and accomplished an athlete as he was, the nerves were intense. In this example, at such a pinnacle experience, initiating a grateful mindset could have helped with seeing what a gift sport is and how lucky he was to be doing something that millions of people can only dream about.

In Opposition to Gratitude

There are three attitudes in direct opposition to gratitude and which, therefore, can be counteracted by it:

- Taking things for granted
- A sense of entitlement
- Resentment

To overcome these attitudes, we need the ability to think outside ourselves, removing ourselves from the centre of the universe and shining the light on everyone and everything that has brought us to our current state of existence.

Taking Things for Granted

The age-old idiom 'you never appreciate what you have until it's gone' is the perfect prompt for us to consider how we might get better at appreciating the things we have before it is too late. If you are not grateful for what you have in life – your family, friends, health, opportunities – then you are taking them for granted. You are likely just assuming that those people and those circumstances will always be there for you, when they may not be. To feel more fulfilled and happier in life, you must be mindful of the things you already have that you can be grateful for. If you have food on the table, running water and a solid roof over your head, you are already far better off than a large percentage of the world's population. Athletes would do well to be mindful of when they are taking their physical and mental health for granted and be grateful for the times when they are in good health.

When True Athlete Project founder, Sam Parfitt, was going through years of poor physical health and multiple surgeries that severely hampered his elite tennis career, he stuck a post-it on his door at those times when he was injury-free which said simply 'You can run!'. This was a reminder to be grateful for what he might otherwise take for granted – the simple pleasure of being able to run without pain.

Most importantly, however, the current universal tendency to take our natural environment for granted is leading us to collectively act far too slowly to address the catastrophic effects of climate change. We must now summon a species-wide sense of deeply experienced gratitude for nature and what it provides for us if we are to avert a dystopian future for humankind.

To begin unravelling the habit of taking things for granted we can start by creating more moments of mindful awareness in our days, noticing the small but important things that happen around us that we are usually too busy to give a second's thought. That way you give your mind and your senses the chance to recognise the richness and beauty of the everyday.

Entitlement

If you believe you are entitled to something then you believe you have no one or nothing to thank if you receive it. You have effectively decided that this was owed to you based entirely on who you are or what you have done. This attitude ignores everything else that has contributed to you receiving or achieving that thing. Given the undeniable influence from a multitude of factors on our every action – our genes, our upbringing, the culture we were born into, the assistance of others, luck – this is a position born of arrogance.

When someone who feels entitled to something does not receive it, it becomes a cause for hysterics and leads to indignation and resentment at the world. An athlete who feels entitled to a victory on the bounds of being the higher ranked player will experience a range of negative and destructive thoughts and emotions if they happen to lose. When the favoured US women's football team lost to Sweden in the quarter-finals of the 2016 Olympic Games in Rio de Janeiro, their goalkeeper, Hope Solo, was scathing in her post-match comments: 'I'm very proud of this team. And I also think we played a bunch of cowards. The best team did not win today, I strongly, firmly believe that … I don't think they're going to make it far in the tournament. I think it was very cowardly. But they won, they are moving on and we're going home.' Solo was subsequently banned from the national team for six months for her disparaging comments which displayed a distinct lack of respect and sportsmanship.

The player who feels entitled to their place in the team will seethe at the indignity and likely ensnare their teammates in their bitterness, if they are not selected. During the 1994 NBA Eastern Conference semi-finals, the legendary Chicago Bulls were tied with the New York Knicks with just 1.8 seconds remaining on the clock. Scottie Pippen had been the Bulls' most dangerous player since Michael Jordan's retirement from basketball, but the coach, Phil Jackson, opted for a play which had Pippen pass the ball to Toni Kukoc to take the all-or-nothing shot. Pippen was so affronted that he wasn't the man chosen to take the shot that he refused to enter the game altogether. He was subbed for another player, and Kukoc made the game-winning shot, but Pippen's actions had shocked and disturbed his teammates – especially since it was so out of character for him. His teammate Steve Kerr said at the time: 'Scottie is one of our favorite teammates and favorite people in the world. … He quit on us. We couldn't believe that happened. It was devastating.'

Resentment

Resentment is a particularly toxic blend of anger and indignation that arises in response to perceived unjust treatment and which can persist indefinitely if not appropriately addressed. It could be triggered by an event as common as a misjudged comment from a teammate, or as serious as consistent mistreatment by a coach, and it often leads to feelings of victimhood and shame which can grow and fester over time.

As Kerry Howells has discussed at length in her 2021 book, *Untangling You – How I Can Be Grateful When I Feel So Resentful*, the interplay between gratitude and resentment has a particularly important role in elite sport. She uses Nelson Mandela's succinct comment – 'Resentment is like drinking poison and hoping it will kill your enemies' – to demonstrate that.

If you harbour feelings of anger, indignation and resentment, ultimately you will only end up hurting yourself. You need to either actively address the source of the resentment, for example speaking to the teammate who caused it, or you must find another way to move past it. If we cannot leave it behind us, Howells demonstrates that the resentment can become like a lens through which we view a more negatively distorted world, and will start to affect our mindset and our relationships. It is, therefore, essential to be able to identify any lingering resentment we hold within ourselves and either address it proactively or find a way to let it go.

One way to proactively combat resentment, either pre-emptively or when you notice it arising within you, is to engage the positive power of gratitude. Gratitude is the antidote to resentment, just as it is with taking things for granted and entitlement. If you become aware of any of these thought patterns then try out one or more of the practices described here.

Gratitude Practices

Imagine you are attending a team meeting on the eve of a really important tournament. The coach waits until everyone is seated and then says, 'Okay, I've got some bad news – it's going to be an absolute disaster tomorrow.' And then they continue: 'Nothing is going to go our way, the referees will be against us, our baggage and food won't arrive on time, we'll be locked out of our changing room until 10 minutes before game time, our star players will get injured due to not having enough warm-up time, so the rest of the team will lose their cool and be off-form, and we'll lose badly.'

This is an exercise that the Stoic philosophy called negative visualisation, essentially preparing yourself for all the bad things that could happen so that you won't be surprised if any of it does come to light, and also so that you can more fully appreciate it when none of what you imagined happens. It is essentially laying the groundwork for not taking for granted all those things, thereby bringing gratitude closer to the surface.

You may not want to spend too much time dwelling on all the bad possibilities in life, but as an exercise to be used every now and then, it can be profoundly effective in changing your mindset in the moment.

Alternatively, you could take the positive route and make a list of all the things that you could be grateful for that you usually take for granted in life. Think of what you have that the poorest and most disadvantaged in the world do not.

Gratitude Journaling

At the end of each day, write down three to five things that you were grateful for that day. This is not just for the big things, but also any of the small things that you would otherwise not have given a second's thought – fresh bread in the morning, a warming sunbeam on bare skin, time spent with family.

As well as increasing your awareness of the many small but significant moments in life, this simple practice of gratitude journaling can give you a more positive outlook on life in general, and improve your self-esteem. Expressing gratitude means you are less likely to hold resentment against others and will reduce levels of social comparison. It has also been shown to counter stress, increase overall well-being and happiness, and even help you sleep better if done right before bedtime.

The One-Minute Recall

Take one minute to write down all the things you are grateful for from the day or week just gone. Once you get going you will realise just how many things happened for you to appreciate. A nice twist to this exercise is to try to come up with the smallest thing that you can be grateful for, raising awareness about what good there has been in your life down to the micro scale.

My own personal version of this exercise comes every night when I climb into bed. I start by bringing to mind how grateful I am to have a warm, dry, comfortable bed to sleep in. I remember that many people in the world are not so lucky. Then I spend a short time drifting on to other things that I feel grateful for at that precise moment. It is a routine I have come to appreciate greatly and even look forward to at the end of each day.

Write a Thank You Letter

Write a letter of gratitude to someone explaining:

1) Why you are grateful to them
2) What impact they have had on your life
3) How your life/experience would be different without them

This can be a handwritten note, an email or a text message, but if you have the opportunity, reading the letter to them in person can significantly increase the meaning and heighten the experience of this gesture.

Showing your appreciation for another person in this way will make their day *and yours*. As an athlete you will have had a great many people volunteering their time and energy to help you get where you are. Acknowledging them is a great exercise in looking up and outside of yourself.

Pay It Forward

If you can recognise a contribution that someone has made to your life – a coach, a teacher, a mentor – which goes beyond any single expression of gratitude, then you can decide (alongside writing to them to say thank you) to pay that gratitude forward and be that person for someone else. The impact of having a caring, supportive, reliable mentor is limitless. Being such a mentor is one of the surest paths to finding meaning in life.

9   Love and Connection

Love vs Fear Reframing

It takes a number of critical factors to win an NBA championship, including the right mix of talent, creativity, intelligence, toughness, and, of course, luck. But if a team doesn't have the most essential ingredient – love – none of those other factors matter.

— Phil Jackson

Fear is a common experience for athletes desperate to prove themselves in competition. It doesn't help that the traditional approach of elite sport ramps up the pressure and therefore the fear by placing an all-consuming focus on the outcome of the sporting contest, be it a match, a fight, a tournament or a league. We cannot control the result, but only parts of our input, and so the most valued part of the performance is out of our hands. This dynamic has the knock-on effect of increasing the fear around losing, around making mistakes, fear of the opponent and fear of one's own emotional response to failing, all of which serve to distract and destabilise us.

As was noted in chapter 2, on compassion, fear can be a powerful motivator, but it comes with a heavy cost which only very few are willing to pay. What we must realise is that this fear-based approach is not the only way to achieve success, nor is it the most effective way. If you can bring the full force of your attention onto your own input – your effort, attitude, values – and place that at the heart of your performance, then you will be able to access greater freedom from claustrophobic thoughts and emotions. This in turn will allow you to perform with more freedom and joy, driven by the love of the endeavour and challenge.

Making the switch from fear to love as the foundation of your motivation and your experience of performance is not easy. The sporting culture and environments that we collectively create must shoulder a lot of the responsibility for replacing fear with love as the driving force for athletic performance. However, there are some key perspective shifts that can have a profound effect when adopted by the individual athlete.

How to Harness the Power of Love in Sport

This model for exploring the role of love in sport was inspired by Jason Dorland, the Canadian Olympic rower and coach who was introduced to you in chapter 1. Dorland experienced first-hand the destructive power of a fear- and ego-based competitive mindset. The Canadian men's eight were defending Olympic champions from the 1984 Olympics, but Dorland and his teammates finished dead last in the 1988 Olympic final in Seoul. Dorland went through a painstaking process of transformation, leading him to adopt an entirely revamped philosophy as the coach of elite rowing teams. He writes about the vision for sport that helped him find this new approach:

> *Imagine a team where love was the foundation of their collective why. Why they played their sport. Why they belonged to a certain team. Why they loved competing. And, where their daily fuel was sourced from a never-ending curiosity in search of the athletic heights for that which they were capable.*

Imagine if athletes felt equally compelled to support the growth and development of their teammates as they did their own. And, even more ambitious, imagine a competitive arena that fostered the celebration of the victors as well as the defeated. Where competition was a synergistic expression of the combined energy of individuals and teams striving for their best performance on the day.

Love is one of the most powerful human forces. To maximise your potential in sport, you can harness this power by aiming to grow your love in the following four areas:

- Your sport
- Yourself
- Your teammates
- Your opponents

Before diving into each area, it is important to note that the term 'love' here denotes a broad and expansive concept. In English we have this one word to describe the full spectrum of experiences and feelings it denotes, whereas in ancient Greece they had seven words to describes different types of love, including romantic love, filial love, the love of friendship, unconditional familial love and self-love. So, when you think about love for teammates or for opponents, do not become bound by notions purely of romantic love.

Love for Your Sport

It is not hard to recognise that athletes who have a great and deep love for their sport will be naturally more motivated, resilient, focused and joyful in their sporting endeavours. Without love for your sport it will become virtually impossible to continue to push yourself, fail and get back up again the numbers of times necessary to make it to the highest levels. Therefore, it is essential to preciously guard and continuously fuel your love for your sport along the way.

The first and perhaps most important step is an awareness-raising exercise.

Write down all the reasons why you love your sport – what you love about yourself and the feelings it gives you when you are practising it.

This is important because during the rough patches which are inevitable in a sporting journey, you may lose track of your love for it. Having this list will act as a simple reminder and can even be used to help you find a helpful perspective to get you through rough patches. Perhaps you wrote that you love your sport because it represents both a physical and mental challenge. In that case, when the going gets tough you can embrace the experience as part of the challenge you love and a part of what makes it so worthwhile to you. If it were easy, you would have given up long ago.

You must not let ambitious outcome-focused goals override your intrinsic love for your sport.

Love for Yourself

This concept is covered fully in chapter 2, treating yourself and others with compassion, and in the self-compassion section that follows in this chapter.

Love for Your Teammates

Humans are innately social animals and we have our roots as a species living in tribes and co-operating for the greater good. The effect of this is that when we do things as a tribe or a team today, we are connected with our ancient past and can create a deep sense of belonging and meaning in the experience. This was described vividly in chapter 4 by Owen Eastwood as the Māori concept of Whakapapa. Likewise doing something for someone else, as opposed to for ourselves, is perhaps the greatest source of fulfilment in life. Muhammad Ali said that being of service to others is the rent we pay for a room on this earth. Archbishop Desmond Tutu popularised the term 'Ubuntu', from the Nguni Buntu language, to describe the philosophy that defined South Africa's transition from racial apartheid to democracy. It means 'the belief in a universal bond of sharing that connects all humanity' or more succinctly 'I am because you are'.

Simon Sinek puts it succinctly: 'If you want to feel happy, do something for yourself. If you want to feel fulfilled, do something for someone else.'

With all this in mind it is no wonder that being a part of a sports team or squad, working day in and day out with others who are similarly ambitious and committed, can be one of the most joyous experiences and can create a whole lot of love. But as with most things, this love can be fragile and must be cultivated with care and attention. The most important thing here is to recognise that the experiences you create with your teammates, both on and off the field of play, will likely form some of the most meaningful memories of all your time in sport. The results and rankings will fade and compress until they are hard to tell apart, while the social bonds and the feeling of unity will remain within you for life.

Increasing your awareness of the importance of the social aspect of sport will help you to place appropriate value on cultivating those relationships. You can start by thinking about flipping the golden rule of '*treat others how you want to be treated*' and instead '*treat others how they want to be treated*'. This is the foundation for building an atmosphere of psychological safety and greater trust between members. For example, instead of assuming that your teammates like to receive feedback in the same way that you do, approach them with a sincere curiosity and ask them if they would like to hear your feedback and if so, when and how would they appreciate hearing it. From there, combined with the powerful emotional experiences of sport, love can flourish.

Recognise, appreciate and respect the differences between the members of your team. Often the best teams are made up of members with very different personalities and perspectives. Michael Jordan, Scottie Pippen and Dennis Rodman could not have been much further apart from each other personality-wise, and yet when they came together in the Chicago Bulls team that was led by Phil Jackson, they became the core of perhaps the most formidable team ever witnessed on a basketball court.

At times when you notice different attitudes or approaches in your teammates it is a great exercise to try and understand where they are coming from, and how they have formed their world view. Perhaps you can identify scenarios where their unique personality brings a particular benefit to the team. Every personality type comes with its own advantages and challenges when situated in a team, the key is to figure out how to maximise the advantages and mitigate any friction.

The British Olympic table tennis player and best-selling author Mathew Syed's book *Rebel Ideas* is all about the value of creating teams of diverse backgrounds, viewpoints and perspectives. His motivation for writing the book speaks volumes about the importance of embracing differences in those around you.

> *My ambition is to leave readers with a sense of why diversity – and specifically cognitive diversity – is central to humanity's progress, and why people who are open to different viewpoints will enjoy more fulfilling and successful lives.*

Love for Your Opponents

He drew a circle that shut me out –
Heretic, rebel, a thing to flout.
But Love and I had the wit to win:
We drew a circle that took him in!

— EDWIN MARKHAM, 'OUTWITTED'

The idea of having love for your opponents is, from my experience, the most challenging of the four areas to understand. While it is easy to understand the importance of respecting an opponent, and lots of athletes are friendly with their competitors, the idea of loving your opponents can seem too extreme. Some might find it difficult to see how a loving approach could help them perform better. So, how can adopting such an attitude actually benefit you as an athlete?

First, consider the competitor who would score 0 out of 10 in *love for their opponents*. They are the type of athlete who sees their opponents as enemies to be crushed, even humiliated, inherently different to themselves, and often with less honourable intentions and methods. Such negative attitudes are incredibly energy-consuming, and the athlete concerned uses a lot of their attention on their opponents as opposed to the performance task at hand. It is important to point out here that the 0 out of 10 does not actually represent a hatred of the opponents but rather a *fear* of them. They are the contemptible *other*, and the most important thing is to prove one's own superiority over them. Underlying this attitude is the fear of what happens if it turns out that *they* are the superior ones. Such an uncomfortable thought sits at the back of the athlete's mind throughout their performance, distracting them and loading on further anxiety. And if the unthinkable actually happens and they lose to their opponent, then the emotional backlash becomes much greater due to such an intensely hostile perspective.

To add further evidence that this is a losing strategy in more ways than one, it is, in fact, founded on a set of false beliefs. This is again where traditional sporting culture has led us down a destructive path, with constant analogies of war, of vicious rivalries, highlighting the differences between teams and athletes so as to heighten the tension and spectacle when they meet. The reality is to be found in the origin of the word 'compete', which was introduced earlier in the book. This *is* the real core of why athletes truly can gain and grow through learning to love their opponents. In order to reach your absolute peak, you need to come up against an opponent who is able to push, challenge and support you there. The level of challenge and the emotional engagement in the endeavour must be just right for you to feel fully engaged and motivated to push yourself to the limit. Without a worthy opponent, you will never reach your potential.

The extraordinary rivalry between Roger Federer and Rafael Nadal stretches back more than 15 years, with over 40 matches played between them at the highest level. Their 2008 Wimbledon final went to five sets and nearly five hours and is widely considered to be the greatest tennis match of all time. There is no doubt that the presence of the other has pushed each one to greater heights of achievement than if they were alone at the very top. Nadal puts it simply, 'If he is playing very good, I have to play unbelievable.' Federer expands on the depth of their relationship, 'It's nice to call one of your biggest rivals a friend. ... I think we really understand each other very well. ... We see life a little differently, but I think we have the ultimate respect for one another.'

Bill Russell, the NBA player with the most championship rings of all time, said in his autobiography, *Second Wind*, that he sometimes secretly rooted for the opposition because if they were doing well it meant he would have a heightened experience.

And in fact, research by Gavin Kilduff, an associate professor of Management and Organisations at the New York University Stern School of Business, has shown that if your rival team performs well one season, then your own team will perform better the following season, and vice versa. Likewise, Kilduff has found that long-distance running athletes will run on average five seconds per kilometre faster if they have a direct rival running in the same race.

If you can make this switch in your perspective and actually begin to appreciate when your opponent is doing well, it will allow you to switch from a threat-oriented state to a challenge-oriented state. The concept that athletes can approach performance in either a challenge or threat state is a relatively recent additions to our understanding of performance psychology. A group of researchers in the UK (Meijen, Turner, Jones and Sheffield) propose that the state an athlete is in will likely determine their sporting performance. Seeing your opponent as a worthy challenger rather than a dangerous threat will help you perform free from fear and anxiety. Your opponent performing well can then be framed as an opportunity to test yourself and perhaps reach higher than ever before.

Another reason why the enemy analogy for opponents is not based on reality is the fact that athletes within the same sport often have far more in common with each other than they may care to admit. Athletes across the world share so much in terms of lifestyle, goals, ambitions and experiences. For those at the elite level, their lives are so taken up by such an uncommon endeavour that it is only their teammates and opponents who can truly understand what they are going through. Most athletes will recognise this by the time they come to the end of their sporting career, when they realise the memories that stand out the most are the experiences they shared with other people – teammates, coaches, opponents etc. It may be part of the reason why mature athletes can perform with greater ease, and less tension, since they have dropped much of the antagonistic element and left behind the associated fear. The earlier an athlete can start to transition to this approach, the sooner they can bring their entire focus onto their own game and game plan, without worrying about the person standing opposite them. Andre Agassi, one of the greatest tennis players of all time, also came around to this realisation, and wanted to share it with the others that came after him. 'I tell the players: You'll hear a lot of applause in your life, fellas, but none will mean more to you than that applause from your peers. I hope each of you hears that at the end.'

Learn to love your opponent for the fact that you rely on each other to create something powerful and meaningful, and also for walking the same path with them through many of the same highs and lows. That shared journey will mean more to you in the long run than any silverware either of you have accumulated.

Developing Self-compassion

Being human is not about being any one particular way; it is about being as life creates you – with your own particular strengths and weaknesses, gifts and challenges, quirks and oddities.

— Kristin Neff

The path to growing your compassion more generally starts with developing greater self-compassion. Here we will introduce some techniques you can use to do that.

Cultivate a Compassionate Inner-dialogue

The goal here is to cultivate the voice inside your head to resemble a good friend and supportive coach rather than a harsh critic. We are all accustomed to being that kind, forgiving friend to others but far less comfortable with responding to our own suffering in the same manner. We have led ourselves to believe either that we deserve the suffering or that it is a helpful motivator for reaching our goals. But motivation based on self-criticism is essentially a fear-based motivation and as we now know, love is a healthier and more powerful motivator than fear.

The first step in cultivating greater self-compassion is always to be able to recognise the moments when you are suffering and what your response is to that suffering. This requires a degree of mindful awareness of what is happening in the present moment and not being swept away in the waves of thought and emotion. For this reason, mindfulness practice is an essential aspect of developing greater self-compassion. You can go back and learn all about mindfulness meditation in the first chapter of Part 3. There is also a specific compassion-focused meditation which we will introduce a bit later on.

To help you become more aware of suffering, in the moment, and prepare yourself to respond more positively, you can start by thinking back to times when you have suffered and been hard on yourself. So, try and think back to such a time – perhaps you made a mistake in a game, your team lost, or you struggled to learn a new technique. Write down a brief description of what caused your suffering and how you felt at the time. Now imagine that it is your best friend or closest teammate in the position you described, and they have shared with you that they feel terrible because of it. What would you say to them? How would you try to make them feel better about the situation and about themselves? In all likelihood your response to your friend would be accepting, warm and forgiving because you know that further suffering would not help them learn or grow and would only make things worse. It may also include some advice about seeing things from a different perspective or looking for the positives of the situation. Now you can use this description as a template for a response to yourself the next time you find yourself in a similar situation. If you can do this exercise for all the times when you tend to be toughest on yourself, then you will have a catalogue of prepared responses that will help you overcome a challenge in the most constructive way possible.

The next method to try takes place in the moment of your own suffering. Bring to mind someone who cares about and loves you – a close friend, teammate or a family member. Now imagine what they would say to help you deal with the situation. If you can speak to them in person or on the phone and describe how you are feeling that is even better. The idea is, over time, to start to internalise their kind, supportive voice until it becomes your own inner voice, responding compassionately in the moment.

Self-compassion Mantra/Cued Response

Another strategy is to be prepared with a set response or mantra, which you repeat either in the moments you become aware of your suffering or self-criticism, or when recalling those moments after the fact.

You can make up your own phrases which are more personal to you, or you can try saying the following to yourself:

- *'This is a moment of suffering'* – Becoming mindfully aware of what is happening for you.
- *'Suffering is a part of life'* – A recognition of the common human experience of suffering.

- *'May I be kind to myself'* – Representing the compassionate response that you want to bring.

Here are some versions of this kind of mantra which are more relevant to sport.

- *'This hurts because I made a mistake.'*
- *'Making mistakes is a part of sport.'*
- *'May I forgive myself so I can move on.'*
- *'I am feeling the pressure.'*
- *'Everyone feels pressure when they care about something.'*
- *'May I continue with courage.'*

Self-compassion Journaling

Journaling is a fantastic tool for reflecting on, expressing and processing emotions and events in your life. There is more about journaling in the section on *reflection* in the next chapter. One way to journal is to recall and note down, at the end of each day, anything you felt bad about, judged yourself for or that caused you emotional pain or suffering.

Try to approach this exercise using the three aspects of self-compassion: mindfulness, common humanity and self-kindness.

Mindfulness – Being aware of what you experienced and how you felt and noting it down in a way that is free of judgement. The idea is simply to notice what arose for you in those moments and look at it with a sense of curiosity and acceptance.

Common humanity – Try to connect your experience to the wider nature of being an athlete or simply human. So, if you felt bad about a performance or the way you behaved, you could note that every athlete has bad days, and to struggle and fail is innately human. There is no development without pushing at the boundary of what we are capable of.

Self-kindness – Write down some words of support and encouragement, drawing on a compassionate voice, either your own or a friend or family member who wants the best for you and knows that you need not suffer simply because of a mistake or a failure of some kind.

Loving Kindness Meditation

This is similar to many other traditional mindfulness meditations, except that it centres on directing benevolent, loving energy towards yourself. It can bring some resistance to the surface at first, since we are not so used to this kind of self-directed love, but with a little practice it can have a profound effect.

You can sit either on a chair with your feet flat on the floor, or on the floor with crossed legs, with straight back and eyes closed. Start by imagining yourself feeling a deep sense of contentment, knowing that you are just right as you are in all your imperfections, feeling an inner peace. Imagine that with each out-breath you are releasing any tension and with each in-breath you are filling yourself up with love.

After a little while repeat the following phrases, or feel free to create your own personalised phrases:

May I be happy,
may I be safe,
may I be healthy, peaceful and strong.

You can take a short break, noticing what feeling arises in you, or simply continue to repeat the three phrases without a break in between.

I will add, on a personal note, that this exercise can feel strange at first. I certainly felt self-conscious to begin with, until I had practised it and eventually realised that for all the awkwardness of speaking to myself like this, I really do want to treat myself with this level of care and love. If this can help me overcome the more negative aspects of my self-talk, then I am happy to indulge in something that feels out of my comfort zone.

The Power of Nature Connectedness

We depend on nature not only for our physical survival, we also need nature to show us the way home, the way out of the prison of our own minds.

— ECKHART TOLLE

Almost everyone now recognises that getting out in nature, breathing fresh air and having some outdoor exercise can do wonders for both physical and mental well-being. Experiencing the great outdoors can increase your creativity, help you de-stress, improve your mood, boost your immune system and even help to combat anxiety and depression.

In the 1980s the Japanese government coined the term 'Shin-rin-yoku', meaning *forest bathing*, to describe the physically and psychologically therapeutic benefits of spending time among trees. Since then, studies have proven that this simple practice can have immense positive effects on the body and mind. In one study of over 20,000 people, conducted by Mathew White at the University of Exeter, it was found that people who spend at least two hours in green spaces per week – either in one go or spread out over multiple visits – were more likely to report good health and mental well-being than those who don't. Richard Louv, who wrote the compelling book *Last Child in the*

Love and Connection

Woods: Saving Our Children from Nature Deficit Disorder, points out, 'When I wrote Last Child in the Woods in 2005...this subject was virtually ignored by the academic world. Now it is approaching and about to pass 1000 studies, and they all point in one direction: Nature is not only nice to have, it's a have-to-have for physical health and cognitive function.'

There is also a growing field of outdoor-, nature- or wilderness-therapy designed to provide a more natural 'therapy room', where body, mind and place can become more interconnected, helping clients disconnect from the fast-paced, technological world they usually inhabit.

Certainly, there is nothing quite like immersing yourself in nature to achieve perspective in life. Modern generations are being increasingly separated from such experiences, and especially from wild nature as opposed to city parks and green suburbs. This unfortunate trend has a great number of detrimental effects; perhaps most serious of all is that without a deeply felt, personal connection to nature, we are far less likely to recognise our innate dependence on our natural environment and, therefore, our responsibility to protect our planet and help it flourish.

Champions for Earth is a movement spearheaded by a group of athletes on a mission: ex-GB rower Dave Hampton, London Olympic gold medallist slalom kayaker Etienne Stott, Lewes FC footballer Katie Rood and Team GB rower Melissa Wilson. Their mission is to use the power and platform of athletes to raise the climate crisis further up everyone's agenda. They identify that it is the values of sport – endeavour, overcoming obstacles, teamwork and a sustained focus over the long term – which are the same that will be needed for us to come together and do what is necessary to avert a global climate catastrophe.

Aside from this vital piece of the puzzle there are countless benefits to getting out of the house and cultivating a deeper

181

connection to the nature around us. We are animals after all, with bodies and minds that have evolved through many thousands of generations to work in harmony and symbiosis with nature. To withdraw permanently into the concrete jungle means to close the door to our biological heritage and hide away from the environments in which we evolved to thrive. Richard Louv coined the term in his book, *Nature-deficit Disorder*, to describe just this type of retreat. To truly understand our own nature and the scale and limits of our role in life, we must be able to escape our modern existence, even if just briefly, and see things through timeless eyes.

To begin to link this concept closer to the world of sport and performance we can start with the *biophilia hypothesis*, which suggests nine ways humans can be considered to have an innate connection to nature. One of those connections is the desire to overcome challenges in nature such as summiting a mountain, surviving for days alone in the wilderness or working as a team to hunt a wild animal. The theory argues that from an evolutionary perspective these were all positive survival characteristics and, therefore, would be carried forward by our genes through the generations. We still see many of these very same challenges being popular today, and in many ways all of modern-day sport has evolved from this form of competition with the self and with nature. Some sports, such as trail running or climbing will maintain a very strong awareness of this link between human and nature, while within other sports this connection will be far less evident.

Here we will introduce some of those benefits which are most relevant to your experience as an athlete, and which are available to anyone who is willing to step out of the river-rush of life and look up and out for but a moment.

The Greatest Perspective

As noted in chapter 5, on awareness, there is a great advantage to being able to zoom out and see things from a wider perspective, especially when you are grappling with stress or anxiety-inducing situations. Humankind has long known the philosophic power that nature holds in showing us how small and insignificant our personal travails are when considered in the context of all life on earth. While it may sound depressing or even frightening, recognising the immensity and timeless beauty of nature more often strikes the beholder in a way that both humbles and empowers them. For our species, being so attuned to a threat to either our ego or our bodies and on macro and micro scale alike, the ability to disengage from the minutiae of life and contemplate our existence on this grander scale can be liberating like no other experience. When it comes down to it, your worries about winning or losing the next match, giving away a foul in the last match, bickering with teammates etc., become comically small-fry when you zoom out in this way.

This level of perspective can be achieved in many ways, from going out hiking or camping in the mountains to looking up at the sky on a clear night or even just watching a nature documentary. For the most transformational experiences one must go out and experience nature first-hand. This is where you gain knowledge and respect for the immensity of nature, and that is hard to replicate without being there and experiencing it for yourself. Once you have had your understanding of your place in the world expanded, then you can draw on this knowledge at times when you are not able to get out into nature, such as during a competition or performance. Adopting this kind of purposeful perspective in moments of anxiety allows you to draw the mind away from unhelpful thoughts to give yourself a chance to breathe easier and refocus on the task at hand.

Discovering Your True Nature

Although it can sound somewhat cliché, there is a reason why so many people choose to go on great outdoor adventures in order to *find themselves*. There is a particular effect that comes from getting far out of your normal environment and routines and into the natural world, one that allows you to notice new things about yourself and your view of life. It is the physical equivalent of the mindful skill of being able to step back and notice the activity of your mind without judgement or attachment. Out in nature, you step back from being on autopilot and become more aware of the everyday commotion of your life without the same moment-by-moment, emotional reactions. This ability to see things afresh can bring a level of quality to your reflections that can help you refine and gain insight into your own values, deeper needs and desires.

As you get closer to nature's rhythms and cycles, for example if you hike by day and sleep in a tent by night, you start to notice the natural responses of your body and mind to those rhythms. In a way, connecting more with nature *is* connecting more with yourself. It is this connection, on the deepest, biological level, which encourages enhanced intuition of the higher, more conceptual parts of yourself.

If you are stuck with some kind of dilemma, then getting out of the hustle and bustle is a great way to find the inner space and perspective that can help you find the right path. This can happen as a result of simply allowing your brain to drop into a lower gear as it gets to focus on a different set of sights and sounds, triggering a range of different psychological connections to be made. The brain accesses degrees of creativity in this way, much like sleeping on a problem moves it into the subconscious as your mind whirrs with new dream-induced patterns and connections.

If you have the chance, a day exploring a local forest or a weekend walking in the hills can give you fresh insight into your own inner workings and also provide you with new angles for thinking or seeing the world. If it is difficult for you to get to the wilderness, even visiting a local park or green space can give you many of the benefits that come with changing scenery and escaping the chaos of city living.

Recharge

In our modern world, our lives are hectic to say the least. 'Busy' is worn as a badge of honour, and with smart phones there is always something nagging for our attention, regularly beeping and vibrating to make sure we are permanently aware of this fact. Stress is an affliction or disease on a worldwide scale and there is no doubt that it is threatening to both health and life. There are all sorts of products and experiences that are marketed for their de-stressing qualities but perhaps none can match an excursion in nature for overall effectiveness. The duration and essence of that excursion will determine the degree of re-charging that could be expected. For example, a 30-minute walk in a park can be the perfect mid-afternoon perk-up to help you refocus on a work task, or a weekend hiking can feel as refreshing as a two-week holiday. If life has really been getting on top of you and stress has been creeping in to your everyday being, then a prolonged retreat to a quieter part of the country, ensconced within natural beauty, simplifying life and your daily routines, could be just what the doctor ordered.

The point is to get out of your usual habits and, as mentioned earlier, allow your mind to settle down, guided by a more natural rhythm. Modern society is not what our minds and bodies were originally adapted for. There is a deep, psycho-emotional relaxation available when returning to the natural environments where our earliest ancestors spent their entire lives for thousands of generations.

Building Relationships and Facilitating Connection

Harking back to the time when our ancestors had to cooperate within their tribe to conquer the challenges of survival, being out in the wilderness has always been an effective facilitator for people to open up, connect and share of themselves. This is a part of the reason for the continued success and popularity of outward-bound style camps, outdoor retreats and team-building courses. The power of such experiences to open us up to form new connections and strengthen the bonds between us may stem from the heightened awareness we get of how much we have in common when all symbols of status are stripped away. In this way nature is a great leveller, and in dismantling existing hierarchies it provides fertile ground for deeper connection.

This notion can be harnessed by teams seeking to come together and create a sense of tribe. Outdoors teambuilding sessions need not include complex physical and mental challenges to solve together. Simply spending time in nature together, perhaps with simple shared tasks such as building shelter and a fire and preparing dinner, can be all that is required to bring people together in a profound way.

In a more everyday sense, if there is tension or growing distance between you and a teammate for example, a walk and talk in a park or woodland is often far more conducive to working things out than a coffee at the local café.

10 Reflection and Conclusion

Reflection

By three methods we may learn wisdom: First by reflection, which is noblest; Second by imitation, which is easiest; Third by experience, which is the bitterest.

— Confucius

Reflection is key to becoming an elite performer. For any person it is the path to gaining greater self-awareness, becoming more focused, taking less for granted and untangling the threads of life. It comes in many forms; both formal and informal reflection can be highly beneficial but given the importance of reflection, we recommend including some formal practices within in your daily or weekly routines.

Reflective practice is an approach to continuous learning which is based in the ability to look back on experiences in a structured way. One of the key rationales of reflective practice is that experience alone does not lead to learning, deliberate reflection is also essential. Melanie Jasper, who wrote the book *Beginning Reflective Practice*, describes a simple model for this process called the ERA Cycle:

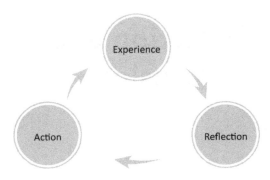

We start with having an experience, which we then reflect on in order to feed into our future actions, which in turn form our next experiences. Within this simple process we can gain a number of important benefits – making sense of an experience, standing back to get a wider perspective, going back over an experience from multiple points of view, deeper honesty from being able to acknowledge things that would have been hard at the time, weighing up the various elements of an experience in a balanced way and gaining clarity from having a bit of distance from the experience.

Here we present a selection of reflection-based exercises, but this is by no means an exhaustive list. These practices involve thinking about

- What we did
- Why we did it like that
- Whether it was successful
- Whether it could have been done any better
- Planning for any changes to our future practice

Check-in, Check-out

One of the simplest and yet most effective tools for reflection is the check-in, check-out score. It can be used any time, for any activity but is especially valuable in relation to athletes' training. Most athletes live busy lives and must often fit in their training around multiple other commitments. Arriving at the training centre directly from school, university or work, it is important to compartmentalise what has gone before in the day and the training which is about to happen. Continuing with the thoughts and worries from the day would not support quality in training, therefore a ritual exercise of separation is needed. The check-in exercise is where you spend just a short time when you arrive at your training venue to look inwards and consider how you are doing, physically and mentally, and give yourself a score out of 10 for how ready and motivated you are for the training. This practice provides a moment of mindfulness, where you are checking in with yourself and your current state, and it allows you to set reasonable expectations for yourself for that training session. If you find you are exhausted, are lacking sleep and have been stressed throughout the day, then you may give yourself a lower score and therefore lower your expectations of how much you can achieve in the session. Perhaps you could try and make it shorter and with more quality or focus on the technical rather than physical aspects. Alternatively, if you arrive full of energy and raring to go, you can set the bar high for training, knowing that you have a lot to give and, therefore, a lot more to potentially gain.

The check-out score, also out of 10, is all about your effort and attitude during the session. How well did you give what you had available to give, bearing in mind your check-in score? This brings into play the 100 per cent approach, whereby, if you rated yourself 6/10 for your check-in then you can still give 6/6 for effort and attitude for that session. It won't be as effective as a 10/10 day but it is still making the most of the situation based on an honest reflection about your state.

Video Analysis

For any athlete, recording and watching video of training or performance is a fertile ground for reflection, analysis and process goal setting. In the words of teaching guru and author of *The Coach's Guide to Teaching*, Doug Lemov: 'Video is an outstanding way to ensure knowledge and understanding outside of and in synergy with what happens in practice.'

When engaged in a sports performance there is often little room for calm and clear reflection during the activity itself. Tiredness and emotion cloud our judgement and intense focus reduces our capacity to think with any real overview or perspective. To analyse our performances as we go, we must rely on the feeling of our technique, and from our narrow, often clouded focus try to determine the effectiveness of our tactical decisions. There are hundreds of cues and messages that we miss due to time and energy constraints. In short, there is a huge amount to learn from our performances that it is difficult or impossible to access in the heat of the moment. Add to this the memory-gap effect, which describes how the result of an action or situation can have a dramatic impact on how positively or negatively we later view it. If a mediocre performance ends in victory, we will be more likely to remember the positives about our performance, and vice versa in the case of a defeat. Leaving everything to memory, therefore, will not optimise our development. The same memory-gap effect can happen with coaches or supporters, so it is not always a fool-proof solution to rely on the accounts of those watching from the sidelines either.

Video footage can provide valuable feedback about your own technique, in the same way that dance studios have mirrored walls that give the dancers 'double' the information from which to improve their technique – from without as well as within.

It can also provide useful tactical insight. Considering stress and fatigue negatively affect cognitive function, it is clear that athletes will often not be processing information perfectly during their activity. Sometimes the mind is so clouded that an athlete is unable to think rationally and, when asked later on, they are unable to recall what they were thinking or even describe what happened in the match. When I do video analysis sessions with fencers, before watching any of the action, I always ask them to start by telling me about the match we are about to watch, from memory. It is fascinating how often their description is a long way from what we come to watch on screen. Even the key moments and turning points of the match turn out to be significantly different when we watch back in the cold light of day. For optimal development, you cannot just leave these experiences to memory. Wherever possible you should review performance video: for example, looking carefully at your actions, noticing changes in tactics from the opponent or any patterns in movement or actions from both sides and making notes of anything you think you can learn from.

Beyond the technical and tactical there is much to be gained from a video by reflecting on what went well, what didn't go so well and what you would do differently the next time. It is often possible to get a decent overview of your strengths and developmental needs at that moment. Reflecting on what was going through your mind at specific moments in the performance can also give insight into the mental side of your game.

From all this available information it is often easy to pinpoint the things that most need to be worked on. The great power of video as a tool for reflection is that it presents you with the clear evidence of the specific points. You don't *need* a coach to tell you what you must do as you have all the buy-in you need to make the necessary changes. However, having a coach or fellow athlete provide a different perspective is very useful when watching video footage.

Journaling

Our brains are not designed to hold and process all the thousands of thoughts and ideas that keep us occupied throughout the day. This is one of the reasons why we can feel stressed and worn out. We are constantly trying to keep up with the agreements and plans we have made as well as everything else on our to-do list, in addition to dealing with our concerns for the future and those around us. Journaling is an incredibly effective a tool for getting the clutter out of our minds, onto paper and therefore into some sort of order. Journaling comes in many forms, so experiment until you find the type that suits you best. It will have a profound impact on all aspects of your life. Here are some of the most popular methods of journaling:

Training journaling – This could be as simple as keeping a gym journal, where you keep a track of all the exercises, loads and reps that you complete as part of your physical training. If you take your strength and conditioning training at all seriously it is essential to keep this kind of journal in order to see in black and white the progress you are making and spot other patterns over time. Improvement is generally incredibly linear with physical training, and the motivation and confidence that comes from seeing your numbers steadily rise is hard to overestimate.

You can also keep a journal regarding your overall training and competition experiences. This can include your check-in, check-out scores, how well you have lived up to your values, your process goals, and any general observations about your physical, psychological and emotional state. There is great awareness to be gained from sorting these kinds of things out in your head by getting them down on paper. Keeping track of your process goals, the aspects of your sport that you are focusing on developing at any given time, can bring the same confidence and motivation as the gym journal, as you see the improvement to specific aspects over time.

Morning/evening journaling – This method of journaling is about setting yourself up for the day by answering a few brief questions about what you hope to achieve, and then reflecting on how things panned out at the end of the day. The habit of setting clear intentions for what you want to achieve will become highly developed on your way to becoming a top athlete, either in the training hall with your process goals, using visualisation before a competition or in exploring your longer-term dreams and goal setting. Setting an intention for how you want your day to go is a wonderfully powerful driver for living the life that you want to lead. Too many people go through their entire day on autopilot, which robs them of a great deal of personal agency and the feeling of being in control of their lives.

Try spending just five minutes each morning answering the following questions:

- What 1–3 things am I grateful for?
- What can I do that would make this a great day?
- What positive affirmation can I say about myself?

These three questions are designed to help you take more notice of the positives in your life, to teach you to take greater responsibility for your own happiness and to define the person you want to be. By doing this exercise every morning you are conditioning your mind to think in these terms, which over time can have a dramatic impact on the way you think and engage with the world.

In the evening you can spend a few minutes reflecting on how things went using the following prompts or making your own.

- What went well today?
- What could I have done to make it even better?

Once again, these questions help to direct our focus towards the positive. As our brains are hardwired to tune in to the negatives it is important to counteract that bias by consciously attending to what is going well and being solution-focused as opposed to problem-focused. This form of questioning also connects with cultivating a *growth mindset* – the desire for constant learning from experiences and understanding that you can always improve on things that you care to work on. This persuasive concept was conceived by a professor of psychology at Stanford University, Carol Dweck, and brought to popular attention by her book *Mindset: The New Psychology of Success*.

Freewriting journaling – This type of journaling is about letting your thoughts, feelings and imagination loose on the page. Writing down everything and anything that comes to mind can be a therapeutic and creative experience. It can take any form you wish, including stream of consciousness, creative/imaginative writing and detailing your experiences and reflections from the day. The point is to get rid of whatever is cluttering up your mind. Freewriting journaling can be a great option for when you are travelling or on holiday and have a bit more time to spend on it, or any period where you feel you want to give space to your creative side and see where your mind leads when you sit down and really follow it.

Dream journaling – Dream journaling can be mysterious, intriguing and also great fun. The method here is simple – keep a notepad beside your bed and as soon as you wake up try to write down everything you can remember from your dreams. If you have multiple dreams, then try to record them all in turn. At first you may find that you can only remember sporadic details, but soon you will recall enough to write paragraphs and perhaps even pages of notes. The daily process of recall sends the signal to your subconscious brain that you want to remember more, and so it comes to pass.

We still know very little about the meaning of dreams, but the consensus is they are a way for the brain to process the events of the day combined with the random firing of neurons that makes for some wacky and vivid dream experiences. You could try to decipher the meaning of your dreams or alternatively just enjoy being able to recall them in ever more clarity and detail.

Your 90th Birthday Thought Experiment

This exercise is similar to the one in chapter 7, where you were asked to imagine a reception held in your honour at the end of your playing career. This time it is about trying to get some perspective on your life as a whole, stretching long into your future beyond playing sport. You can think of it as a kind of future reflective exercise, in that you are imagining yourself reflecting on your life experiences from the latter years in your life.

In the experiment, you imagine that you are sitting alone on the morning of your 90th birthday thinking back on your long, fulfilled life. Write down some of the things that come to mind. These could include:

- What were the major themes in your life? Think about this in terms of work, your relationships with family and friends, the hobbies and interests you enjoyed and your health.
- What were the most important and fulfilling aspects of your journey?
- Where and how did you make the biggest impact?
- What advice, if any, would you give to your younger self?

Create a Personal Motto, Credo or Oath

Spirit in motion

— MOTTO OF THE PARALYMPIC GAMES

Mottos, credos and oaths are creative ways to powerfully encapsulate your approach to specific parts of your life, or your life as a whole. They can help you to make a habit of the mindset that you wish to cultivate, to remind you of your purpose and focus, and to exemplify the overall tone of your philosophy. As with anything, the more visible and available something is, the more likely it is to stick with you. Just as it helps to have your core values displayed somewhere you'll see them on a daily basis, the same goes for the kind of attitude you want to bring to life. Many people like to put up pictures or posters with their favourite quotes or sayings they believe in or know will lift their mood.

It can be even more powerful, however, to put some work into creating your own, personalised versions of these motivational sayings.

Motto

A motto is a short phrase which sums up something important to you that can be recalled at relevant moments to help bring about a desired state of mind or sense of perspective.

For example, the traditional Buddhist saying 'This too shall pass' may be recalled in moments of turbulence to gain perspective and see that everything is just a phase. Another famous saying 'Who dares, wins' could be employed to instil courage at moments of vulnerability. Winning in this case does not have to represent winning the sporting contest but could instead be understood as winning the personal challenge.

You could consider the moments where you are most often or most intensely challenged and try to come up with your own motto that describes succinctly how you want to be in that moment.

Credo

An athlete rational credo is a more detailed description of the kind of mindset and approach that you wish to bring to your sporting life. Based on a psychological model called Rational Emotive Behaviour Therapy (REBT) and adapted by a leader in that field, Dr Martin J. Turner, the athlete rational credo is a series of personalised, rational statements which describe an ideal, resilient response to challenge and adversity. Within the framework of REBT, athletes are susceptible to a number of irrational beliefs which should be addressed in order to create a more logical, less stress-inducing way of thinking about their experience and performance.

The irrational beliefs fit into the following categories:

Category	Example
Rigid and extreme demands	'I want to win this match and therefore I must win'
Awfulising	'If I don't win this match it will be absolutely terrible'
Frustration intolerance	'I could not tolerate it if I lost this match'
Depreciation	'If I lose this match it means I am a complete failure'

When creating your own athlete rational credo it can help to address each of these irrational belief categories in turn and craft a rational, more resilient response. Examples of such rational responses are:

Category	Example
Flexible and non-extreme preference	'I want to win this match but that does not mean that I must win'
Anti-awfulising	'If I don't win this match it will be bad but not terrible'
Frustration tolerance	'If I lost this match it would be tough, but I could tolerate it'
Acceptance	'If I lose this match it does not make me a complete failure. I am fallible just like all human beings'

This gives you a single example for each category of both irrational and rational beliefs, so the task is to think about your own situation and the times when you have fallen into the irrational belief trap, and then consider what a more helpful, rational response would be if that moment arises again. This could be around selection for a team, the way your coach or teammates treat you, your own skill development or trajectory in your sport, the recognition you receive from those around you, or countless other areas.

The approach advocated by REBT helps us to realise the maxim of Stoic philosophy, that it is not events themselves that cause our emotional reactions but our beliefs about those events. The better we can be at promoting within ourselves rational, helpful beliefs, the happier and healthier our lives will be.

Oath

An oath is a solemn promise regarding your own behaviours and actions. The most well-known oaths are the Hippocratic Oath, recited by new physicians; the oath to tell the truth in a court of law; and the oath of political office, such as that the president of the United States must recite. There is also of course the Olympic oath, which is recited by a representative of all the athletes, at the opening ceremony of the Games:

> *In the name of all the athletes we promise to take part in these Olympic Games, respecting and abiding by the rules and in the spirit of fair play. We all commit ourselves to sport without doping and cheating. We do this, for the glory of sport, for the honour of our teams and in respect for the Fundamental Principles of Olympism.*

An oath has a ceremonial, almost spiritual aspect to it, and therefore, can feel more binding than a motto or a credo. Creating your own oath also gives you a chance to unleash a bit more of your creative, poetic side.

You could choose to create your oath based on your own core values, having followed the values exercise in chapter 7. Just remember not to promise perfection in thought or act, as that is not humanly achievable, and can only lead to disappointment.

For inspiration, the True Athlete Oath could be:

> *I promise to follow the True Athletes' path of training mind, body and spirit*
> *cultivating mindfulness, embracing my own humanity and recognising it in others.*
> *I choose to grow my love for myself, my competitors, my sport and those around it,*
> *so that I may know that I have done my best, and my community may benefit too.*
> *I am an aware athlete, a scholar athlete, a compassionate athlete,*
> *I am a True Athlete.*

Final Thoughts

Now it is over to you. You can decide what to keep and what to leave from everything you have read in this book. The True Athlete Philosophy was created through the collaboration of a special collection of people with deep personal experiences of sport from a wide variety of angles, and a passion to help unleash the true positive power of sport. That is not to say that this philosophy applies equally to everyone, or that individual athletes will find each element equally attractive. This is meant as a starting point, an inspiration for you to create your own sporting philosophy, intentionally. We certainly hope that the higher purpose of sport we proposed in chapter 1 resonates with you and will serve as a solid foundation on which you can be confident that whatever is built will have integrity and add value to the world. There are many virtues to choose from that are not described in this book that could contribute to the same higher purpose. Do not get too wrapped up in trying to adhere to the absolute letter of this philosophy, because that is not the point, and it would probably end up being more stressful than beneficial. Instead, try to use this as a catalyst to being more purposeful in how you go about sport and your wider life, becoming better at choosing your responses rather than simply reacting. Looking around you and taking a real interest in the things you see.

There may be elements that challenged your beliefs about what is important, relevant or practical for an ambitious athlete, that would be perfectly understandable. We believe that there is *something* valuable in this Philosophy for everyone, and likely far more than the traditional approach to sport would have us believe. A realistic goal would be to turn up those dials of self-compassion, gratitude, responsibility etc. by 10 per cent. This is a way to think about things as you try to develop some of the attributes that resonate in this book. Consider having a dial for each quality and see if you can turn the dial up by 10 per cent, and then notice what difference that makes. If it works for you and you like the effect, then you can go for another 10 per cent. Sometimes, with the help of some revelatory information or experience, you can turn up a dial significantly in one go.

This happened to me when I began working with Katie Warriner, my sport psychologist, in the run-up to the London 2012 Olympics. She felt the need early in our work together to point out that losing a match does not necessarily have to lead to devastation on my part. As simple as that sounds, I had never once heard that it doesn't *have* to be painful to lose – that you can commit every bit as much passion and energy to the performance but without falling into a chasm if the result goes the wrong way. This revelation led me to explore and adopt a whole new, values-based approach to my sport, which resulted in being able to perform with far greater freedom and joy. Ultimately it allowed me to perform on the biggest stage, the Olympics, with heart pounding through my chest, and cherishing every second.

This kind of paradigm shift may sound extreme, but it is not uncommon, especially among athletes who are open-minded and on the lookout for ways to learn and understand more about their experience. The reason this type of revelation is possible at all is that traditional sport culture is built on so many out-of-date theories and practices. The ideas in this book at times contrast with the commonly accepted norms of elite sport. For example, traditionally, resilience has been thought to be built by toughening up and developing character through gruelling hardship and humiliation. But here we have tried to present a different view of resilience, built on self-compassion, mindfulness, embracing our inherent vulnerability, and developed through practice. Not only does this offer a better path to resilience, it also supports other spheres of life and can foster a spiritual connection to ourselves and those around us.

That brings us back to the underlying purpose of this entire philosophy – cultivating *True Athletes* who develop themselves through sport in all ways to be of service to society.

The butterfly on the cover of this book reflects this profound transformation of the individual and the effect of that transformation on the wider world. It is the logo of the True Athlete Project and captures the essence of the organisation: 'To transform the world, one true athlete at a time'. The butterfly is a universal symbol of transcendence, awakening and peace. It also symbolises 'the butterfly effect' (the theory by Edward

Lorenz that small changes to weather conditions on one side of the world can lead to huge weather effects on the other), the unknown power of our actions, and how our growth both on and off the field of play truly matters and can be drawn upon to make a difference to others. The logo honours the inspirational figure of Muhammad Ali, at whose centre in Louisville The True Athlete Project took flight. Ali represents the epitome of the humanitarian athlete, acutely aware of the world around him and the platform he had to make a difference, founded on the immense sporting talents with which he held the world spellbound.

Finally, the orange and the blue in the original logo represent the yin and the yang, the calm and the fire, the strength and the sensitivity needed by athletes to achieve excellence in sport and in life.

These final thoughts sum up what we hope this book and the Philosophy described within it will achieve – to be the start of a ripple effect, both within you, the individual athlete, and out into the world as more people realise this need for sport to live up to its higher purpose.

Values List

Acceptance
Accomplishment
Accountability
Accuracy
Achievement
Adaptability
Alertness
Altruism
Ambition
Amusement
Assertiveness
Attentive
Awareness
Balance
Boldness
Bravery
Brilliance
Calm
Candour
Capable
Careful
Certainty
Challenge
Charity
Cleanliness
Clear
Clever
Comfort
Commitment

Common sense
Communication
Community
Compassion
Competence
Concentration
Confidence
Connection
Consciousness
Consistency
Contentment
Contribution
Control
Conviction
Cooperation
Courage
Courtesy
Creation
Creativity
Credibility
Curiosity
Decisive
Decisiveness
Dedication
Dependability
Determination
Development
Devotion
Dignity

Discipline
Discovery
Drive
Effectiveness
Efficiency
Empathy
Empower
Endurance
Energy
Enjoyment
Enthusiasm
Equality
Ethical
Excellence
Experience
Exploration
Expressive
Fairness
Family
Famous
Fearless
Feelings
Ferocious
Fidelity
Focus
Foresight
Fortitude
Freedom
Friendship

Fun
Generosity
Genius
Giving
Goodness
Grace
Gratitude
Greatness
Growth
Happiness
Hard work
Harmony
Health
Honesty
Honour
Hope
Humility
Imagination
Improvement
Independence
Individuality
Innovation
Inquisitive
Insightful

Inspiring
Integrity
Intelligence

Intensity
Intuitive
Irreverent
Joy
Justice
Kindness
Knowledge
Lawful
Leadership
Learning
Liberty

Logic
Love
Loyalty

Mastery
Maturity
Meaning
Moderation
Motivation
Openness
Optimism
Order
Organization
Originality
Passion
Patience
Peace
Performance
Persistence
Playfulness
Poise
Potential
Power
Present
Productivity
Professionalism
Prosperity
Purpose

Quality
Realistic
Reason

Recognition
Recreation
Reflective
Respect
Responsibility
Restraint
Results-oriented
Reverence
Rigour
Risk
Satisfaction

Security
Selfless
Self-reliance

Sensitivity
Serenity
Service
Sharing
Significance
Silence
Simplicity
Sincerity
Skilfulness
Skill
Smart
Solitude
Spirit
Spirituality
Spontaneous
Stability
Status
Stewardship
Strength
Structure
Success
Support
Surprise
Sustainability

Talent
Teamwork
Temperance

Thankful
Thorough
Thoughtful
Timeliness
Tolerance
Toughness
Traditional
Tranquillity
Transparency
Trust
Trustworthy

Truth
Understanding
Uniqueness

VALUES LIST

Unity
Valour
Victory
Vigour

Vision
Vitality
Wealth
Welcoming

Winning
Wisdom
Wonder

Thanks

There were a great many people who contributed in big and small ways to the contents and writing of this book. There is no way it would have become fit for publication without their contributions, so I am eternally grateful to all these people who gave so generously. First and foremost, I must acknowledge and thank the most important people in my life:

Helena, my wife, who has been by my side, both metaphorically and literally, throughout this whole part of my journey. It was also Helena who provided the spark for me to think more critically about the role of sport in society, which led me, in turn, to TAP and to a whole new world of possibility and passion. Then there are Cora and Wyatt, who, together with my wife, represent the deepest purpose of my life. They help me see and understand so many of the concepts raised in this book – mindfulness, compassion, gratitude, living by your values, etc – in such clear and practical terms.

Next, I would like to thank Sam, the person who, with superhuman dedication, laid the groundwork and set the vision that brought all of this into being. It has been a pleasure to do so much of this work in partnership with you. Likewise, the people who have come into the TAP family, the volunteers, trustees and our wonderful and inspiring mentors and mentees. Surrounded by such people makes everything feel hugely worthwhile and exciting.

Thanks to Andy, who created Sequoia to be a pioneer for a new style of author-centred publishing – a most honourable mission. You have been absolutely true to your word and I have hugely appreciated your support (and lightning-fast response times) every step of this journey. Thanks also to Jenny Volich for the care and attention you gave to editing the book.

There were two people who went above and beyond in their level of engagement and attention to detail when I sent them early drafts to ask for feedback: Cath Bishop and David Buist. You blew me away with the many hundreds of comments and suggestions, and I can't thank you enough.

A number of people were kind enough to read early drafts and give feedback, and each has had a significant impact on the book: Clare Halsted, Josie Perry, Georgina Parfitt, Daniel Sigurdsson, Jason Dorland, Troels Thorsteinsson, Anthony Turner, Noora Ronkainen, Todd Iarussi, Danny Cullinane, Pam Boteler and Mike Johnson. Please know that you have all left your mark on this collective piece of work.

I was lucky enough to be able to draw on experts within the TAP network who I could run specific sections by: Nicole Gabana, James 'Stevo' Stephenson, Amber Mosewich, Sam Cooley, Martin Turner and Stuart Carrington. Your oversight has given me much needed confidence that I was not making any disastrous omissions or errors.

And finally, I would like to credit a few key people, and their podcasts, who have inspired and shaped so much of my thinking around the contents of this book. Dan Abrahams, *The Sport Psych Show*; Simon Mundie, *Don't Tell Me the Score*; Tim Ferriss, *The Tim Ferriss Show*; and Sam Harris, *The Making Sense Podcast*. If you have enjoyed the themes in this book, then I can highly recommend subscribing to all of these podcasts.

References

Chapter 1

AFL, Marngrook – https://aiatsis.gov.au/blog/afls-aboriginal-origins.

Amy Tinkler – https://www.itv.com/news/2020-10-07/amy-tinkler-id-give-up-my-olympic-medal-if-i-could-change-what-gymnastics-has-done-to-me.

Aristotle – *Nicomachean Ethics*. London: G. Bell and sons, 1889.

Asif Kapadia – https://economictimes.indiatimes.com/news/sports/everywhere-they-have-own-version-of-maradona-asif-kapadia-british-filmmaker/articleshow/71471634.cms?from=mdr.

Barack Obama – *A Promised Land*. Crown Publishing Group, 2020.

British gymnastic lawsuit and Rachel Pinches quote – https://www.theguardian.com/sport/2021/feb/26/british-gymnastics-faces-class-action-lawsuit-from-17-alleging-abuse-jennifer-pinches?CMP=Share_iOSApp_Other.

Cath Bishop – *The Long Win*. Practical Inspiration Publishing, 2020.

Choi Suk-hyeon – https://www.bbc.com/news/world-asia-53263178.

Dalai lama – https://www.facebook.com/DalaiLama/posts/interdependence-is-a-fundamental-law-of-nature-even-tiny-insects-survive-by-coop/10152653910687616/.

Deci & Ryan – https://selfdeterminationtheory.org/theory/.

IBU report – https://www.insidethegames.biz/articles/1103507/ibu-external-review-report-findings.

Icarus – Film by Bryan Fogel.

Jason Dorland – www.yourmindset.ca.

Jigoro Kano – *Mind Over Muscle*. Kodansha International, 2005.

John Wooden – *On Leadership*. Mcgraw-Hill, 2005.

Jonathan Haidt – *The Happiness Hypothesis*. Basic Books, 2006.

Journals of the American Medical Association – https://jamanetwork.com/journals/jama/fullarticle/2645104.

REFERENCES

Kelly Holmes – https://www.theguardian.com/sport/2019/mar/13/kelly-holmes-mental-health-happiness-self-harming-podcast-interview.

Lacrosse – https://worldlacrosse.sport/about-world-lacrosse/origin-history/#:~:text=Lacrosse%20was%20started%20by%20the,around%20the%20western%20Great%20Lakes.

Marcus Aurelius – https://www.goodreads.com/quotes/1320634-the-body-and-its-parts-are-a-river-the-soul.

Michael Bennett – *Things that make White People Uncomfortable*. Haymarket Books, 2018.

Michael Phelps – The Weight of Gold documentary.

National Alliance for Youth Sport survey – www.nays.org.

Olympic charter – https://www.olympic.org/news/the-olympic-charter.

Pierre De Coubertin – https://www.researchgate.net/publication/239788268_Pierre_de_Coubertin's_vision_of_the_role_of_sport_in_peaceful_internationalism.

Qatar abuses – https://www.amnesty.org/en/latest/campaigns/2019/02/reality-check-migrant-workers-rights-with-two-years-to-qatar-2022-world-cup/.

Rio Olympic violations – http://www.childrenwin.org/wp-content/uploads/2015/12/DossieComiteRio2015_ENG_web_ok_low.pdf.

Robert Emmons – Personal Goals, Life meaning and virtue, wellsprings of a positive life. https://www.psychology.hku.hk/ftbcstudies/refbase/docs/emmons/2003/53_Emmons2003.pdf.

Rugby Players Association survey – https://www.skysports.com/rugby-union/news/12321/11574137/over-60-per-cent-of-retired-rugby-players-face-mental-health-challenges-say-rpa.

Simon Sinek TED Talk – https://tinyurl.com/8bvuk3d.

Survey on public trust in sport, The Brewery at Freuds – https://medium.com/the-brewery/public-trust-in-sport-insight-b48e109c174f.

Swiss Gymnastics – https://www.insidethegames.biz/index.php/articles/1103629/swiss-gymnastics-independent-report.

UK children's physical activity statistic – https://www.sportengland.org/news/active-lives-children-and-young-people-survey-academic-year-201819-report-published.

Venus Williams – https://tinyurl.com/54rhvdtm.

Chapter 2

Abraham Lincoln – https://www.goodreads.com/quotes/565665-i-am-not-bound-to-win-but-i-am-bound.

Amber Mosewich – Self-compassion in sport and exercise. https://www.researchgate.net/publication/341921073_Self-Compassion_in_Sport_and_Exercise.

Crista Cullen – https://www.bbc.com/sport/42871491.

Dalai Lama – https://www.dalailama.com/.

David Hamilton – *The 5 Side-Effects of Kindness.* Hay House, 2017.

David Hamilton – https://drdavidhamilton.com/how-kindness-is-contagious/.

Diego Mentrida – https://www.instagram.com/diegomentrida/.

Ibtihaj Muhammad – https://tinyurl.com/uwcb9cut.

IOC Celebrate Humanity, Adversary – https://theolympians.co/tag/celebrate-humanity/#:~:text=You%20are%20my%20adversary%2C%20but,Instead%2C%20I%20will%20honor%20you.

Kristin Neff – https://self-compassion.org/.

Neff and Vonk – https://self-compassion.org/wp-content/uploads/publications/NeffVonk.pdf.

Paul Gilbert – https://www.compassionatemind.co.uk/.

Professional Players Federation – https://www.ppf.org.uk/ppf-org-uk/_img/images/doc/PPF%20Past%20Player%20Research%202018.pdf.

Traumatic Stress study – https://self-compassion.org/wp-content/uploads/publications/SCandPTSD.pdf.

Chapter 3

FIFA FBI Investigation – https://en.wikipedia.org/wiki/2015_FIFA_corruption_case.

FIFA FBI Investigation – https://www.bbc.com/news/world-europe-32897066.

USADA – https://www.theguardian.com/sport/2012/oct/11/armstrong-usada-sophisticated-doping-scheme.

Muhammad Ali – https://tinyurl.com/y5fsuzas.

Saracens – https://www.bbc.com/sport/rugby-union/51168926.

Transparency International football survey – https://www.transparency.org/en/press/most-fans-dont-believe-gianni-infantinos-first-year-has-won-back-trust-in-f.

Chapter 4

Andre Agassi – *Open.* Harper Collins, 2009.

Arthur Ashe – https://www.goodreads.com/quotes/9743989-start-where-you-are-use-what-you-have-do-what.

British Fencing model – https://www.britishfencing.com/athlete-development-programme-zone/leadership-models/.

Daniel Goleman – *Emotional Intelligence: Why it Can Matter More than IQ.* Bantam Books, 1995.

Daniel Goleman – *Working with Emotional Intelligence.* Bloomsbury Publishing, 2009.

Eugenio Monti – https://en.wikipedia.org/wiki/Eugenio_Monti.

Jones, Paull, Erskine – https://www.researchgate.net/publication/10995362_The_impact_of_a_team's_aggressive_reputation_on_the_decisions_of_Association_football_referees.

Marcus Rashford open letter – https://www.theguardian.com/football/2020/jun/15/protect-the-vulnerable-marcus-rashfords-emotional-letter-to-mps.

Marcus Rashford – https://www.theguardian.com/politics/2020/jun/16/boris-johnson-faces-tory-rebellion-over-marcus-rashfords-school-meals-call.

Megan Rapinoe – https://edition.cnn.com/2020/08/05/football/megan-rapinoe-uswnt-activism-spt-intl/index.html.

Nick Kyrgios – https://www.theguardian.com/sport/blog/2019/aug/28/nick-kyrgios-us-open-tennis.

Owen Eastwood – *Belonging.* Quercus, 2021.

Rafael Nadal – https://www.tennis365.com/atp-tour/rafael-nadal-lays-into-disrespectful-nick-kyrgios-after-dramatic-acapulco-match/.

RepTrak – https://www.firstpost.com/sports/federer-most-trusted-respected-after-mandela-in-the-world-survey-88642.html.

Robert K. Greenleaf – *Servant Leadership - A Journey into the Nature of Legitimate Power and Greatness.* Paulist Press, 2002.

Roger Federer – https://www.nzherald.co.nz/sport/the-moments-that-transformed-roger-federer-from-a-boy-into-a-man/2RLPGD2VUEKBZCY4ECEBGF67RQ/.

Ruth Bader Ginsberg – https://www.youtube.com/watch?v=nLGLtUXXR1E&feature=emb_logo.

Stuart Carrington – *Blowing the Whistle: The Psychology of Football Refereeing.* Dark River, 2019.

Uncle Ben – https://tinyurl.com/ppn3u2mp.

Chapter 5

Alzheimer's association – https://www.alz.org/aaic/overview.asp.

Athleten Deutschland – https://athleten-deutschland.org/.

Colin Kaepernick – https://www.denverpost.com/2020/06/07/colin-kaepernick-timeline/.

Colin Kaepernick – https://www.skysports.com/nfl/news/12118/12170048/colin-kaepernick-how-taking-a-knee-started-after-nfl-quarterback-met-nate-boyer.

Dave Zirin – https://www.thenation.com/article/archive/enduring-importance-activist-athlete/.

Deja Young – https://www.teamusa.org/News/2020/May/15/From-Mental-Institution-To-Paralympic-Gold-Deja-Young-Recounts-Her-Harrowing-Mental-Health-Journey.

Global Athlete – https://globalathlete.org/.

Ivan Lawler – http://www.worldpaddleawards.com/organisation/ivan-lawler-british.

Jigoro Kano – *Mind over Muscle*. Kodansha International, 2005.

Johnny Wilkinson – https://www.shortlist.com/news/jonny-wilkinson-success-mental-health-rugby-england-interview.

Jon Kabat-Zinn – https://tinyurl.com/ms8x7nrk.

Lebron James – https://amp.theguardian.com/sport/2021/feb/27/lebron-james-zlatan-ibrahimovic-criticism?__twitter_impression=true.

Miyamoto Musashi – *A Book of 5 Rings: The Classic Guide to Strategy*. Gramercy, 1988.

Nicole Gabana – https://www.researchgate.net/publication/326614036_Attitude_of_Gratitude_Exploring_the_Implementation_of_a_Gratitude_Intervention_with_College_Athletes.

Nicole Gabana – https://www.researchgate.net/publication/333710843_Gratitude_in_Sport_Positive_Psychology_for_Athletes_and_Implications_for_Mental_Health_Well-Being_and_Performance.

Origin of 'winning' – https://www.etymonline.com/word/win#:~:text=win%20(n.),attested%201862%2C%20from%20the%20verb.

Psychologically Informed Environment – https://www.homeless.org.uk/sites/default/files/site-attachments/Creating%20a%20Psychologically%20Informed%20Environment%20-%202015.pdf.

Vijnana – https://www.learnreligions.com/vijnana-449563.

Viktor Frankl – *Man's Search for Meaning*. WOW Publishings, 2020.

Zlatan Ibrahimovic – https://www.youtube.com/watch?v=GX1bhLpgsvM.

Chapter 6

Amishi Jha – http://www.amishi.com/lab/mbat_project/.

Andi Puddicombe – https://www.headspace.com/meditation/quotes.

APA mindfulness article – https://www.apa.org/monitor/2012/07-08/
ce-corner#:~:text=The%20researchers%20concluded%20that%20
mindfulness,decreases%20anxiety%20and%20negative%20affect.

Buddha – https://www.realbuddhaquotes.com/drop-by-drop/.

Charles Duhigg – *The Power of Habit*. Random House Trade Paperbacks,
2014.

Dalai Lama – https://responsiveuniverse.me/2012/11/20/if-every-8-year-
old-in-the-world-is-taught-meditation-we-will-eliminate-violence-from-
the-world-within-one-generation-dalai-lama/.

Holistic Life Foundation – https://www.theguardian.com/us-news/2016/
nov/06/baltimore-school-students-meditation-patterson-high.

Jules Evans – https://thoughteconomics.com/the-role-of-philosophy-in-life/.

Martin Seligman – https://ppc.sas.upenn.edu/people/martin-ep-seligman.

Mihaly Csikszentmihaly – *Flow – The Psychology of Optimal Experience*.
Harper Perennial Modern Classics, 2008.

Monkey Mind – https://www.pocketmindfulness.com/understanding-
monkey-mind-live-harmony-mental-companion/.

Mindful Sport Performance Enhancement – https://www.
mindfulsportperformance.org/.

Operation Wellness Warrior Program – https://www.davidlynchfoundation.
org/veterans.html.

Russell Okung – https://www.espn.com/nfl/story/_/id/9581925/seattle-
seahawks-use-unusual-techniques-practice-espn-magazine.

Seattle Seahawks – https://tinyurl.com/shc94fc3.

Soren Gordhamer – https://tinyurl.com/shc94fc3.

Steve Peters – https://chimpmanagement.com/the-chimp-model/.

Time magazine – http://content.time.com/time/subscriber/
article/0,33009,2163560,00.html.

Tom Brady – https://www.theguardian.com/sport/2021/feb/01/tom-brady-
super-bowl-retirement-age-nfl-football.

Chapter 7

Brene Brown – *The Power of Vulnerability – Teachings on Authenticity,
Connection and Courage*. Sounds True; Unabridged edition, 2012.

Brene Brown Ted Talk – https://www.ted.com/talks/brene_brown_the_
power_of_vulnerability?language=en.

Douglas, K., & Carless, D. (2006). Performance, discovery, and relational
narratives among women professional tournament golfers. *Women in
Sport & Physical Activity Journal*, *15*(2), 14.

Gandhi – https://www.goodreads.com/quotes/50584-your-beliefs-become-your-thoughts-your-thoughts-become-your-words.

Houltberg, Benjamin J., Wang, Kenneth T., Qi, Wei, & Nelson, Christina S. (2018). Self-narrative profiles of elite athletes and comparisons on psychological well-being. *Research Quarterly for Exercise and Sport,* 89(3), 354–360, DOI: 10.1080/02701367.2018.1481919.

Kaya Turski – https://www.cbc.ca/playersvoice/entry/how-do-you-forgive-yourself-for-failing-at-the-olympics.

Kierkegaard – https://www.goodreads.com/quotes/15578-to-dare-is-to-lose-one-s-footing-momentarily-not-to.

Lebron James – https://www.becomeempower3d.com/blog/making-more-than-an-athlete-more-than-a-phrase.

Lizzie Simmonds – https://lizziesimmonds.com/2019/02/27/crossing-the-identity-chasm/.

Marcus Rashford – https://www.theguardian.com/football/2021/jan/17/marcus-rashford-the-making-of-a-food-superhero-child-hunger-free-school-meals.

Simon Sinek – *Start with Why.* Penguin Books Limited, 2011.

Chapter 8

Cicero – https://www.goodreads.com/quotes/72368-gratitude-is-not-only-the-greatest-of-virtues-but-the.

Epictetus – https://dailystoic.com/control-and-choice/.

Ethan Kross – episode #127. https://thesportpsychshow.libsyn.com/.

Frances Houghton – *Learnings From Five Olympic Games.* 2020.

Hope Solo – https://www.theguardian.com/football/2016/aug/12/hope-solo-sweden-cowards-olympics-football-rio-2016.

Hope Solo – https://nationalpost.com/sports/olympics/hope-solo-suspended-from-u-s-soccer-team-for-saying-they-lost-to-a-bunch-of-cowards-at-rio-2016.

Jacob Hansen, Christoffer Henriksen & Carsten Hvid Larsen – *Mindfulness and Acceptance in Sport.* Taylor & Francis, 2019.

Jenna Woolven – https://www.linkedin.com/pulse/giving-up-struggle-why-letting-go-control-gives-you-more-woolven/.

Kerry Howells – Howells, K. (2021). *Untangling You: How Can I be Grateful When I Feel So Resentful.* Melbourne: Major Street Publishing.

Mathew Pinsent – https://www.the42.ie/annie-vernon-interview-4608672-Apr2019/.

Nelson Mandela - Howells, K. (2021). *Untangling You: How Can I be Grateful When I Feel So Resentful.* Melbourne: Major Street Publishing.

Steve Kerr – https://eu.usatoday.com/story/sports/nba/2020/05/10/the-last-dance-scottie-pippen-wouldnt-change-protest-knicks/3101349001/.
Teri Mckeever – https://www.youtube.com/watch?v=LruJtdyq1IQ.

Chapter 9

Andre Agassi – *Open*. Harper Collins, 2009.
Bill Russell – *Second Wind: The Memoirs of an Opinionated Man*. Simon & Schuster; Reprint edition, 1991.
Biophilia Hypothesis – *The Biophilia Hypothesis*, Steven Kellert & Edward Wilson. Island Press, 2013.
Champions for Earth– https://championsforearth.com/.
Eckhart Tolle – https://www.facebook.com/Eckharttolle/posts/we-depend-on-nature-not-only-for-our-physical-survival-we-also-need-nature-to-sh/10156125677436217/.
Edwin Markham – http://holyjoe.org/poetry/markham.htm.
Gavin Kilduff – https://leadersinsport.com/performance/rival-can-push-teams-athletes-greater-heights/.
Jason Dorland – https://yourmindset.ca/the-last-dance-i-sure-hope-so/.
Kristin Neff – https://www.goodreads.com/quotes/7114577-being-human-is-not-about-being-any-one-particular-way.
7 Greek words for love – https://www.wellandgood.com/greek-words-for-love/.
Mathew White – https://www.nature.com/articles/s41598-019-44097-3.
Mathew Syed – *Rebel Ideas*. John Murray, 2019.
Meijen, Turner, Jones, Sheffield- https://www.frontiersin.org/articles/10.3389/fpsyg.2020.00126/full.
Muhammad Ali – https://www.goodreads.com/quotes/50646-the-service-you-do-for-others-is-the-rent-you.
Phil Jackson – *Eleven Rings*. Penguin Books, 2014.
Rafael Nadal – https://www.atptour.com/en/news/federer-nadal-10-best-quotes.
Richard Louv – https://tinyurl.com/9dafyxu2.
Richard Louv – *Last Child in the Woods: Saving our children from nature deficit disorder*. Algonquin Books, 2005.
Roger Federer – https://tennis-shot.com/roger-federer-reveals-about-his-relationship-with-rafael-nadal/.
Roger Federer – https://www.tennisworldusa.org/tennis/news/Rafael_Nadal/83762/roger-federer-it-is-only-love-and-respect-between-me-and-rafael-nadal-/.
Simon Sinek – https://www.youtube.com/watch?v=jDIZS4IQlQk.

Shinrin-Yoku – https://www.nationalgeographic.com/travel/article/forest-bathing-nature-walk-health.
Ubuntu – https://en.wikipedia.org/wiki/Ubuntu_philosophy.

Chapter 10

Athlete Olympic Oath – https://www.olympic.org/faq/games-ceremonies-and-protocol/what-is-the-olympic-oath.
Butterfly effect – https://en.wikipedia.org/wiki/Butterfly_effect.
Carol Dweck – *Mindset: The New Psychology of Success*. Ballantine Books, 2007.
Confucius – https://www.goodreads.com/quotes/83-by-three-methods-we-may-learn-wisdom-first-by-reflection.
Doug Lemov, *The Coach's Guide to Teaching*. John Catt Educational Ltd, 2020.
Martin J Turner – Turner, M. J. (2020, August 6). The rational pursuit of excellence. The Smarter Thinking Project. https://thesmarterthinkingproject.com/the-rational-pursuit-of-excellence-athletes/.
Melanie Jasper – *Beginning Reflective Practice*. Nelson Thornes, 2003.
Paralympic motto – https://tinyurl.com/5an9e97j.

REFERENCES

About the Author

Laurence Cassøe Halsted is a two-time Olympic fencer who competed for Team GB in the London 2012 and Rio 2016 Olympics. After retiring from competitive sport, Laurence became Performance Director for the Danish Fencing Federation. He joined The True Athlete Project in 2016 where he is currently Director of Mentoring as well as Consultant on TAP's various other programmes and projects, all with an ambition of creating a more compassionate world through sport.

Laurence lives with his wife and two children in Copenhagen, Denmark.

Index

purpose of, 107
qualities of, 106
second arrow parable and,
116–17
self-compassion and, 176, 178
significance of, 105–8
Mindfulness-Based Attention
Training, 105
Mindful Sport Performance
Enhancement, 112
Mindset (Dweck), 194
Monti, Eugenio, 75–6
morning/evening journaling,
193–4
Mosewich, Amber, 41
motivation, 5, 18, 35, 37, 94, 130
common humanity and, 39
love and, 167, 176
self-compassion and, 42
self-kindness and, 38
Muhammad, Ibtihaj, 45
Muhammad Ali Center
(Louisville), xiv
Mumford, George, 40
Musashi, Miyamoto, 95

Nadal, Rafael, 72, 173
Nash, Tony, 75
National Alliance for Youth Sport,
4–5
nature connectedness, power of,
180–2
building relationships and
facilitating connection and,
186–7
discovery of true nature of
oneself and, 184–5
greatest perspective and, 183–4
recharge and, 185–6
Nature-deficit Disorder (Louv), 182
Neff, Kristin, 36, 41, 42, 45, 175
negative visualisation, 163

nervousness, xii, 53, 82, 96, 113,
151, 154
NFL, 8
Nielsen, Thor, 87
Norenberg, Danielle, 144

Obama, Barack, 3
Okung, Russell, 114
Olympic Charter, on vision of
sport, 3–4, 9
Olympics (2000) (Sydney), 49
Olympics (2012) (London), xi,
47, 92
Olympics (2016) (Rio), xii, 8–9,
45, 47, 152
one-minute recall and gratitude,
164
openness, 41, 106, 116, 202
athlete identity and, 137, 140,
141
love and connection and, 171,
186
Operation Warrior Wellness
programme, 115
optimism, xiii, 41, 59, 155
originality, xiii, 48, 90, 186

Paralympics (2016) (Rio), 93
Parfitt, Sam, xiii, xiv–xv, 159
passion, xiv, 11, 14, 97, 122, 134,
200, 202
patience, 31, 105
pay it forward attitude and
gratitude, 165
peace, 34, 87, 143, 179, 202
True Athlete Philosophy and,
15, 19, 20, 26
peaceful protests, significance of,
97
performance narrative, 126, 127
persistence, 36, 134, 161
perspective

defusion as, 153–5
Effort & Attitude system
    (E&A), 144–5
    rating system, 148–50
effort as, 145–6
gratitude as, 155–9
    entitlement and, 160–1
    journaling, 163
    one-minute recall and, 164
    pay it forward attitude and,
        165
    practices, 162–3
    resentment and, 161–2
    taking things for granted
        and, 159–60
    thank you letter writing
        and, 164
    preparation and, 143–4
    REBT and, 199
STOP process, 117–18
Stott, Etienne, 181
stress, 156, 185
subjectivity, of virtues, 33
success, 14–18, 22, 56, 119, 126
    awareness and, 86, 88, 94
    compassion and, 30, 34, 44
    love and connection and, 166,
        171, 186
    responsibility and, 65, 66, 74–6
    Stoic approach and, 143, 144
Suk-hyeon, Choi, 6
support, 38, 66, 115, 165, 202
    awareness and, 84, 86, 92–5,
        100
    love and connection and, 168,
        173, 176, 177, 179
    True Athlete Philosophy and, 4,
        5, 9, 10, 21, 24
sustainability, 12, 19, 42, 109, 181
Swiss Gymnastics Federation, 6
Syed, Mathew, 171

Tae Kwon Do, 20
Teagle, James, 48
Team Danmark, 151
teamwork, 46, 181c
Tewaaraton, 21
thank you letter writing and
    gratitude, 164
Thorsteinsson, Troels, 58
thought experiment, 132–3
timelessness, 114, 182, 183
Time Magazine, 105
Tinkler, Amy, 16
Tolle, Eckhart, 180
toughness, 21, 94, 129, 202
    compassion and, 36, 42, 46
    love and connection and, 166,
        169, 177
traditional athlete traits, 29–30
training journaling, 192–3
tranquillity, 23
Transparency International, 57
True Athlete; *see also individual
    entries*
    definition of, 24–6
    Oath, 200
    objective of, 11–12
    responsibility to make positive
        impact for, 76
    significance of, 12–13, 63
    virtues of, 31–3
True Athlete Project, The (TAP)
    Mentoring Programme,
        143–4
    significance of, xiii–xv, 77
    vision of, xv
trust, 52, 64, 73, 79, 170
    integrity and, 51
    public, 6, 57, 62
    responsibility and, 64
truth, viii, 82, 199
Turner, Martin J., 197